Oppression and Liberty

Simone
Weil

Oppression and Liberty

Translated by Arthur Wills and John Petrie

London and New York

Oppression et liberté was first published 1955
by Gallimard, Paris

English edition first published 1958
by Routledge & Kegan Paul

First published in Routledge Classics 2001
by Routledge
2 Park Square, Milton Park, Abingdon, Oxon OX14 4RN
711 Third Avenue, New York, NY 10017 (8th floor)

Routledge is an imprint of the Taylor & Francis Group, an informa business

Translation © 1958 Routledge & Kegan Paul

Typeset in Joanna by RefineCatch Limited, Bungay, Suffolk

British Library Cataloguing in Publication Data
A catalogue record for this book is available from the British Library

ISBN 10: 0-415-25560-0 (cased)
ISBN 10: 0-415-25407-8 (limp)

ISBN 13: 978-0-415-25560-8 (cased)
ISBN 13: 978-0-415-25407-6 (limp)

CONTENTS

Contents

PROSPECTS

Are we heading for the proletarian revolution?

I would not give a farthing for
the mortal whom empty hopes can
set afire.
SOPHOCLES. Ajax, 477–8

The long-foreseen moment has arrived when capitalism is on the point of seeing its development arrested by impassable barriers. In whatever way we interpret the phenomenon of accumulation, it is clear that capitalism stands essentially for economic expansion and that capitalist expansion has now nearly reached the point where it will be halted by the actual limits of the earth's surface. And yet never have there been fewer premonitory signs of the advent of socialism. We are in a period of transition; but a transition towards what? No one has the slightest idea. All the more striking, therefore, the carefree security with which we settle down in this transition period as though it were a definite stage, so much so that considerations concerning the crisis of the system have almost everywhere become commonplaces. Certainly, we can always go on believing that socialism will arrive the day after tomorrow, and make a duty or a virtue of this belief; so long as we go on taking, day by day, the day after tomorrow to mean the next day but one after today, we shall be sure not to be disappointed; but such a state of mind is difficult to distinguish from that of those worthy people who believe, for instance, in the Last Judgment. If we want to traverse this sombre age in manly fashion, we shall refrain, like the Ajax of Sophocles, from letting empty hopes set us afire.

Throughout history men have struggled, suffered and died to free the oppressed. Their efforts, when they did not remain sterile, have never led to anything except the replacing of one oppressive régime by another. Marx, who had observed this, thought he was able to demonstrate scientifically that things were different in our day, and that the struggle of the oppressed would now lead to a true emancipation, not to a new oppression. It is this idea, which we have preserved as an article of faith, that we need to examine afresh, unless we mean systematically to close our eyes to the events of the past twenty years. Let us spare ourselves the disillusionments of those who, having fought for Liberty, Equality, Fraternity, discovered one fine day that what they had got was, as Marx says, Infantry, Cavalry, Artillery. But they at any rate were able to draw some lesson from the surprises of history; sadder is the lot of those who perished in 1792 or 1793, in the street or on the frontiers, fully convinced that with their lives they were purchasing the freedom of mankind. If we are to perish in the battles of the future, let us do our best to prepare ourselves to perish with a clear vision of the world we shall be leaving behind.

The Paris Commune was an example not only of the creative power of the working-class masses in movement, but also of the fundamental impotence of a spontaneous movement when it comes to fighting against organized forces of repression. August 1914 marked the bankruptcy of proletarian mass organizations, both on the political and the trade-union planes, within the framework of the system. From then onwards it became necessary to abandon once and for all the hopes placed in this mode of organization not only by the reformists, but by Engels. On the other hand, October 1917 ushered in new and radiant prospects. At last the means had been found of combining legal with illegal action, the systematic labours of disciplined militants with the spontaneous seething of the masses. All over the world communist parties were to be formed to which the Bolshevik party would pass on its knowledge and technique; they were to replace social democracy, already described by Rosa Luxemburg, in August 1914, as a "stinking corpse", and very soon to disappear from the stage of history; and they were to seize power within a very short time. The political régime set up spontaneously by the workers of Paris in 1871, then by those of St. Petersburg in 1905, was to become solidly entrenched in Russia and so on to embrace the entire civilized world. Of course, the crushing of the Russian Revolution by the brutal intervention of foreign imperialism might blast these brilliant prospects; but, unless such a thing occurred, Lenin and Trotsky were certain of introducing into history precisely this particular series of transformations and not any other.

Fifteen years have elapsed. The Russian Revolution has not been crushed. Its enemies, both abroad and at home, have been vanquished. And yet nowhere on the surface of the globe—including Russia—are there any soviets; nowhere on the surface of the globe—including Russia—is there any communist party properly so called. The "stinking corpse" of social democracy has continued for fifteen years to infect the political atmosphere, which is hardly the action of a corpse; if at last it has largely been swept away, this has been the work of fascism, not of the Revolution. The régime born of October, which had either to expand or perish, has for fifteen years accommodated itself very well to the boundaries set by its national frontiers; its role abroad now consists, as events in Germany clearly demonstrate, in stifling the revolutionary activities of the proletariat. The reactionary bourgeoisie have at last perceived that it has very nearly lost all force of expansion, and are wondering whether they could not now make use of it by arranging defensive and offensive alliances with it with a view to future wars (cf. the *Deutsche Allgemeine Zeitung* for 27th May). The truth is that this régime resembles that which Lenin thought he was setting up in so far as it excludes capitalist property almost entirely; in every other respect it is the exact opposite. Instead of genuine freedom of the press, there is the impossibility of expressing a free opinion, whether in the form of a printed, typewritten or hand-written document, or simply by word of mouth, without running the risk of being deported; instead of the free play between parties within the framework of the soviet system, there is the cry of "one party in power, and all the rest in prison"; instead of a communist party destined to rally together, for the purposes of free co-operation, men possessing the highest degree of devotion, conscientiousness, culture, and critical aptitude, there is a mere administrative machine, a passive instrument in the hands of the Secretariat, which, as Trotsky himself admits, is a party only in name; instead of soviets, unions and co-operatives functioning democratically and directing the economic and political life of the country, there are organizations bearing, it is true, the same names, but reduced to mere administrative mechanisms; instead of the people armed and organized as a militia to ensure by itself alone defence abroad and order at home, there is a standing army, and a police force freed from control and a hundred times better armed than that of the Tsar; lastly, and above all, instead of elected officials, permanently subject to control and dismissal, who were to ensure the functioning of government until such time as "every cook would learn how to rule the State", there is a professional bureaucracy, freed from responsibility, recruited by co-option and possessing, through the concentration in its hands of all economic and political power, a strength hitherto unknown in the annals of history.

The very novelty of such a régime makes it difficult to analyse. Trotsky persists in saying that we have here a "dictatorship of the proletariat", a "workers' State", albeit with "bureaucratic deformations", and that, as regards the necessity for such a régime to expand or perish, Lenin and he were mistaken only over the time-scale. But when an error in degree attains such proportions we may be permitted to think that an error in kind is involved, in other words a mistake touching the actual nature of the régime of whose conditions of existence a definition is being attempted. Besides, to call a State a "workers' State" when you go on to explain that each worker in it is put economically and politically at the complete disposal of a bureaucratic caste, sounds like a bad joke. As for the "deformations", this term, singularly out of place in the case of a State all of whose characteristics are exactly the reverse of those theoretically associated with a workers' State, seems to imply that the Stalin régime is a sort of anomaly or disease of the Russian Revolution. But the distinction between the pathological and the normal has no theoretical validity. Descartes used

to say that a clock out of order is not an exception to the laws governing clocks, but a different mechanism obeying its own laws; in the
same way we should regard the Stalin régime, not as a workers' State
out of order, but as a different social mechanism, whose definition is to
be found in the wheels of which it is composed and which functions
according to the nature of those wheels. And, whereas the wheels of a
workers' State would consist of the democratic institutions of the working class, those of the Stalin régime consist exclusively of the various
parts of a centralized administrative system on which the whole economic, political and intellectual life of the country is entirely
dependent.

For such a régime, the dilemma "expand or perish" not only is no
longer valid, but no longer even has any meaning; the Stalin régime,
considered as a system of oppression, is no whit more contagious than
was the French Empire for France's neighbours. The view according to
which the Stalin régime constitutes a mere transition, either in the
direction of socialism or in that of capitalism, also seems arbitrary. The
oppression of the workers is evidently not a step in the direction of
socialism. The "bureaucratic and military machine" which constituted,
in Marx's eyes, the real obstacle in the way of a continuous march
towards socialism through the simple accumulation of successive
reforms, has no doubt not lost this property, seeing that contrary to
what was foreseen, it has survived the capitalist economy. As for the
restoration of capitalism, which could only take place as a sort of
colonization, this is not at all impossible, in view of the greed that
characterizes all imperialisms and of the economic and military
weakness of the U.S.S.R.; however, the rivalries between the various
imperialisms have, so far, prevented the ratio of forces from being
overpoweringly against Russia. At all events, the Soviet bureaucracy is
in no sense tending towards a renunciation of its powers, so that the
term "transitional" would in any case be wrong. There is nothing
which entitles us to assert that the Russian State bureaucracy is preparing the ground for any domination other than its own, whether that of
the proletariat or that of the bourgeoisie. Actually, all the embarrassed
explanations by which the militants trained under Bolshevism try to
escape from having to recognize the fundamental falsity of the prospects advanced in October 1917 are based on the same preconceived

notion as were those prospects themselves, namely, on the assertion, regarded as a dogma, that there can at the present time be only two types of State, the capitalist State and the workers' State. This dogma is brutally denied by the development of the régime deriving from the October Revolution. No workers' State has ever yet existed on the earth's surface, except for a few weeks in Paris in 1871, and perhaps for a few months in Russia in 1917 and 1918. On the other hand, for nearly fifteen years now, over one-sixth of the globe, there has reigned a State as oppressive as any other which is neither a capitalist nor a workers' State. Certainly, Marx never foresaw anything of this kind. But not even Marx is more precious to us than the truth.

The other outstanding phenomenon of our time, that is to say fascism, fits no more easily into the categories of classical Marxism than does the Russian State. On this subject, too, of course, there are clichés serving as an escape from the painful obligation of having to think. Just as the U.S.S.R. is a "workers' State" more or less "deformed", so fascism is a movement of the lower-middle classes, based on demagogy, and constitutes "the bourgeoisie's last card before the triumph of the Revolution". For the degeneration of the workers' movement has led the theorists to represent the class struggle as a duel, or a game between actively conscious partners, and each social or political event as a manoeuvre by one of these partners—a conception that has no more to do with materialism than has Greek mythology. There exist small groups of high financiers, big industrialists and reactionary politicians who consciously defend what they take to be the political interests of the capitalist oligarchy; but they are as incapable of preventing as they are of arousing a mass movement like fascism, or even of directing it. In point of fact, they have at times assisted it, at times fought against it; they have tried vainly to turn it into a docile instrument and have ended by surrendering to it. Certainly it is the presence of an exasperated proletariat which, for them, makes this surrender a lesser evil. Nevertheless, fascism is something altogether different from a card in their hands. The brutal manner in which Hitler dismissed Hugenberg, as if he were a domestic servant, in spite of Krupp's protests, is significant in this respect. Nor must it be forgotten that fascism definitely puts an end to that interplay of parties born of the bourgeois régime which no bourgeois dictatorship, even in time of war, had ever yet suppressed; and that it has installed in its place a political régime more or less the same in structure as that of the Russian régime as defined by Tomsky: "One party in power and all the rest in prison." We may add that the mechanical subordination of the party to the leader is the same in each case, and guaranteed in each case by the police.

But political sovereignty is nothing without economic sovereignty; which is why fascism tends to approach the Russian régime on the economic plane also, by concentrating all power, economic as well as political, in the hands of the Head of the State. Here, however, fascism comes up against capitalist property, which it has no intention of destroying. There lies a contradiction whose outcome it is difficult to foresee. But just as the mechanism of the Russian State cannot be explained merely by "deformations", so this fundamental contradiction in the fascist movement cannot be explained merely by demagogy. What is certain is that, whereas Italian fascism only attained to the concentration of political power after many long years which exhausted its impetus, national-socialism, which reached the same result in less than six months, still contains immense reserves of energy, and tends to go very much farther. As a report issued by an important German concern clearly shows—*L'Humanité* quoted it without perceiving its significance—the bourgeoisie is alarmed at the threat of State control, and, indeed, Hitler has set up State organs with sovereign power to condemn workers or owners to ten years' hard labour and to confiscate businesses.

Vain efforts are made, in the attempt to bring national-socialism at all costs within the Marxist framework, to find at the heart of the movement a disguised form of the class struggle, between the instinctively socialist rank and file and the leaders standing for the interests of big business whose aim is to hoodwink the masses by skilful demagogy. To begin with, nothing entitles us to declare with certainty that Hitler and his lieutenants, whatever their ties with monopolistic capitalism, are mere instruments in its hands. And then, above all, the orientation of the Hitlerite masses, though violently anti-capitalist, is by no means socialist, any more so than the demagogic propaganda of the leaders; for the object is to place the national economy, not in the hands of the producers grouped into democratic organizations, but in the hands of the State apparatus. Now, although it is a long time since the influence of the reformists and the Stalinists made us forget the fact, socialism is the economic sovereignty of the workers and not of the bureaucratic and military machine of the State. What is called the "national-Bolshevik" wing of the Hitler movement is therefore in no sense socialist. It follows that the two political phenomena which dominate our time can neither of them find a place in the traditional picture of the class struggle.

The same applies to a whole series of contemporary movements springing from the post-war period and remarkable for their affinity with both Stalinism and fascism. Such, for example, is the German review *Die Tat*, which groups together a band of young and brilliant economists, is extremely close to national-socialism, and regards the U.S.S.R. as the model for the future State, save in the matter of the abolition of private property; it is at present advocating a military alliance between Russia and Hitlerite Germany.

In France, we have a few groups, such as that of the review *Plans*, in which a like ambiguity is found. But the most significant movement of this kind is that technocratic movement which is said in a short space of time to have spread over the whole of the United States. We know that it advocates, within the limits of a closed national economy, the abolition of competition and markets and an economic dictatorship exercised in sovereign fashion by technicians. This movement, which has often been compared to Stalinism and fascism, has all the greater scope in that it appears to be not without influence over the group of intellectuals at Columbia who are at present advising Roosevelt.

Such ideological trends are something absolutely new, giving its own character to our time. For the rest, the present period, however confused and rich in political trends of all kinds, new and old, seems to lack only that very movement which, according to the forecasts, was to constitute its essential feature, namely, the struggle for the economic and political emancipation of the workers. There are, to be sure, scattered here and there and divided by obscure quarrels, a handful of old-time trade unionists and sincere communists; there are even a few small organizations that have preserved wellnigh intact the socialist watchwords. But the ideal of a society governed in the economic and political sphere by co-operation between the workers now inspires scarcely a single mass movement, whether spontaneous or organized;

and that at the very moment when, on every hand, there is nothing but talk of the bankruptcy of capitalism.

Faced with this state of things, we are obliged, if we wish to look reality in the face, to ask ourselves whether that which is to take the place of capitalism is not to be a new system of oppression, instead of the free association of producers. I should like in this connection to submit an idea, purely as a hypothesis, for examination by the comrades. We can say, to put it briefly, that up to the present mankind has known two principal forms of oppression, the one (slavery or serfdom) exercised in the name of armed force, the other in the name of wealth thus transformed into capital; what we have to determine is whether these are not now being succeeded by a new species of oppression, oppression exercised in the name of management.

The mere reading of Marx clearly shows that already, half a century ago, capitalism had undergone profound changes of a nature to transform the very mechanism of oppression. This transformation has become more and more pronounced between Marx's death and the present time, and at a particularly accelerated tempo during the post-war years. We already see in Marx that the phenomenon which makes capitalism what it is, namely, the buying and selling of man-power, has become, in the course of the development of big industry, a subordinate factor in the oppression of the working masses; the decisive moment, so far as the worker's reduction to slavery is concerned, is no longer the moment when, on the labour market, he sells his time to the boss, but the moment when, having scarcely crossed the threshold of the factory, he is swallowed up by the undertaking. We know Marx's terrible utterances on this subject: "In craftsmanship and fabrication by hand, the worker makes use of the tool; in the factory, he is at the service of the machine." "In the factory there exists a dead mechanism, independent of the workers, which incorporates them as living cogs." "It is only with mechanization that the inversion [of the relationship between the worker and the conditions of work] becomes a reality that can be grasped in the technique itself." "The separation of the spiritual forces of the process of production from manual work, and the transformation of the former into forces of oppression exercised by capital over labour, is fully accomplished . . . in large-scale industry built up on the basis of mechanisation. The detail of the individual destiny . . . of the worker working at the machine disappears like some squalid trifle before the knowledge, the tremendous natural forces and the collective labour which are crystallized in the machine system and go to make up the owner's power."

If we leave out hand-fabrication, which can be regarded as a mere transition, we may say that the oppression of the wage-earners, based, to begin with, essentially on the relationship between property and exchange in the days of small workshops, has become, with the advent of mechanization, a mere aspect of the relationships involved in the very technique of production. To the conflict set up by money between buyers and sellers of labour has been added another conflict, set up by the very means of production, between those who have the machine at their disposal and those who are at the disposal of the machine. The Russian experiment has shown that, contrary to what Marx too readily assumed, the first of these conflicts can be eliminated without entailing the disappearance of the second. In capitalist countries, both conflicts coexist, and this coexistence gives rise to considerable confusion. The same men sell themselves to capital and serve the machine; on the other hand, it is not always the same men who own the capital and run the business.

As a matter of fact, there was still, not so long ago, a class of work-men who, although wage-earners, were not simply living cogs in the service of the machines, but on the contrary carried out their work while using machines with as much freedom, initiative and intelli-gence as the craftsmen who wields his tool; these were the skilled workmen. This class of workmen, which, in each industrial concern, constituted the essential factor in production, has been more or less swept away by rationalization. Nowadays, a machine-setter has the job of setting a certain number of machines according to the requirements of the work to be carried out, and the work is accomplished under his orders by specialized hands able to handle one type of machine, and one only, always using identical movements, in which intelligence plays no part. Thus a factory is at present divided into two clearly separated camps—those who execute the work without, strictly speaking, taking any active part in it, and those who direct the work without executing anything. Between these two groups composing the personnel of an industrial concern, the machine itself forms an impassable barrier. At the same time, the development of the system of limited companies has created a barrier—less precise, it is true—between those who manage the business and those who own it. A man like Ford, who is both a capitalist and the managing director of a business, nowadays seems to us a survival from the past, as the American economist Pound has remarked. "Industrial concerns", writes Palewski in a book published in 1928, "tend more and more to get out of the hands of those captains of industry who were the original owner-managers of the business. . . . The age of the tycoons tends more and more to become a thing of the past. We are entering a period that has been called the age of the technicians of management, and these technicians are as far removed from the engineers and the capitalists as are the workmen. The head is no longer a capitalist who owns the business; he has been replaced by a board of technicians. We still live on that past which is so close to us, and the mind has a certain difficulty in grasping this development."

Here again we are dealing with a phenomenon which Marx had already perceived. But, whereas in Marx's time the managing staff of the undertaking was hardly more than a team of employees at the service of the capitalists, nowadays, vis-à-vis the small shareholders reduced to the role of mere parasites and the big capitalists mainly concerned with financial manipulations, the "technicians of management" form a distinct social stratum whose importance tends to increase and which absorbs in various ways a considerable proportion of the profits. Laurat, in his book on the U.S.S.R., analysing the mechanism of the exploitation exercised by the bureaucracy, remarks that "the personal consumption of the bureaucrats"—a consumption disproportionate, generally speaking, to the value of the services rendered by them—"effected regularly and as a fixed charge" operates almost independently of capital reserve requirements which figure under the heading "profits" only after "running costs", that is to say the needs of the bureaucracy, have been covered; and he compares this system to the capitalist system under which "capital reserve requirements come before the payment of dividends". But he forgets that, although capital reserves come before dividends, the "running costs" in capitalist countries, exactly as in the U.S.S.R., come before the placing to capital reserve. Never has this phenomenon been as striking as today, when undertakings on the verge of bankruptcy, having sacked a host of workmen and working at a third or a quarter of their productive capacity, preserve almost intact a managerial staff composed of a few directors drawing fat fees and clerks who are ill-paid, but whose numbers are out of all proportion to the rate of production. Consequently, there are grouped round the undertaking three quite distinct social strata—the workers, passive instruments of the undertaking, the capitalists whose authority rests on an economic system in process of decay, and the managing personnel who rely, on the contrary, on a technique whose development only keeps on increasing their power.

This rise of the bureaucratic element in industry is only the most characteristic aspect of an altogether general phenomenon. The essential thing about this phenomenon is a specialization increasing from day to day. The transformation that has taken place in industry, where skilled workmen capable of understanding and handling many types of machine have been replaced by specialized unskilled hands automatically trained to serve one type of machine only, is the image of a development which has occurred in every field. If the workers are becoming more and more lacking in technical knowledge, the technicians are not only often pretty ignorant of working practice, but furthermore their proficiency is in many cases limited to a quite restricted field; in America, they have even set about producing specialized engineers—just like ordinary unskilled men—in a certain category of machines, and, what is significant, the U.S.S.R. has hastened to copy America in this respect. Moreover, it goes without saying that the technicians are ignorant of the theoretical basis of the knowledge which they employ. The scientists, in their turn, not only remain out of touch with technical problems, but are furthermore entirely deprived of that general view of things which is the very essence of theoretical culture. One could count on one's fingers the number of scientists throughout the world with a general idea of the history and development of their particular science: there is none who is really competent as regards sciences other than his own. As science forms an indivisible whole, one may say that there are no longer, strictly speaking, scientists, but only unskilled hands doing scientific work, cogs in a whole their minds are quite incapable of embracing.

Examples could be multiplied. In almost all fields, the individual, shut in within the bounds of a limited proficiency, finds himself caught up in a whole which is beyond him, by which he must regulate all his activity, and whose functioning he is unable to understand. In such a situation, there is one function which takes on a supreme importance, namely, that which consists simply in co-ordinating; we may call it the administrative or bureaucratic function. The speed with which bureaucracy has invaded almost every branch of human activity is something astounding once one thinks about it. The rationalized factory, where a man finds himself shorn, in the interests of a passive mechanism, of everything which makes for initiative, intelligence, knowledge, method, is as it were an image of our present-day society. For the bureaucratic machine, though composed of flesh, and of well-fed flesh at that, is none the less as irresponsible and as soulless as are machines made of iron and steel. The whole evolution of present-day society tends to develop the various forms of bureaucratic oppression and to give them a sort of autonomy in regard to capitalism as such. That is why it is our duty to define this new political factor more clearly than Marx was able to do.

As a matter of fact, Marx had perceived the force of oppression constituted by bureaucracy. He had seen perfectly well that the true obstacle to emancipatory reforms is not the system of exchange and of property, but "the bureaucratic and military machine" of the State. He had quite understood that the most disgraceful blot to be wiped out by socialism is not wage-earning, but "the degrading division between manual and intellectual work", or, according to another formula, "the separation of the spiritual forces of labour from manual labour". But Marx did not ask himself whether this was not a case of an order of problems independent of the problems presented by the operation of the capitalist economy properly so called. Although he had witnessed the division between property and management in capitalist enterprise, he did not ask himself whether the administrative function, in so far as it is permanent, might not, independently of all monopoly over property, give rise to a new class of oppressors. And yet, though one can see very well how a revolution can "expropriate the expropriators", one cannot see how a method of production founded on the subordination of those who do the work to those who co-ordinate could do otherwise than produce automatically a social structure of which the distinguishing mark is the dictatorship of a bureaucratic caste. Not but what one can imagine a control and a system of rotation whereby equality in the State as well as in the actual process of industrial production could be restored; but, in point of fact, when a social stratum finds that it has any kind of monopoly in its hands, it preserves that monopoly until the very foundations on which it rests have been undermined by the historical process.

It was in this way that feudalism fell, not through the pressure of the lower orders themselves taking possession of armed force, but by the substitution of trade for war as the principal means of domination. In the same way, the social stratum of which the mark is the exercise of administrative functions will never consent, whatever the legal system of property may be, to allow the working masses access to those functions, to teach "every cook how to rule the State", or every unskilled worker how to run the business. Every system characterized by the domination of one class over another in effect corresponds, historically, to the distinction between one dominant social function and one or several subordinate functions. Thus, in the Middle Ages, production was something subordinate as compared to the defence of the fields by armed force; at the next stage, production, having become essentially industrialized, found itself subordinated to distribution. Socialism will exist when the dominant function is productive labour itself; but this cannot happen as long as a system of production continues in which labour as such finds itself subordinated, by means of the machine, to the function consisting in co-ordination of labour. No expropriation can solve this problem, against which the heroism of the Russian workers was shattered. Abolishing the division of men into capitalists and proletarians does not in the least imply that "the separation of the spiritual forces of labour from manual labour" must disappear, even progressively.

The American technocrats have drawn an enchanting picture of a society in which, with the abolition of the market, technicians would find themselves all-powerful, and would use their power in such a way as to give to all maximum leisure and comfort possible. This idea reminds us, by its utopianism, of that of enlightened despotism which our forefathers cherished. All exclusive, uncontrolled power becomes oppressive in the hands of those who have the monopoly of it. And we can already see very clearly how, within the capitalist system itself, the oppressive action of this new social stratum is taking shape. In the field of production, the bureaucracy, an irresponsible mechanism, brings about, as Laurat has observed in connection with the U.S.S.R., on the one hand an unlimited parasitism, and on the other an anarchy which, in spite of all the "plans", is at least equal to that occasioned by capitalist competition. As for the relationships between production and consumption, it would be useless to hope that a bureaucratic caste, whether Russian or American, would restore them by subordinating the first to the second.

Every human group that exercises power does so, not in such a way as to bring happiness to those who are subject to it, but in such a way as to increase that power; it is a matter of life and death for any form of domination whatsoever. As long as production remained at a primitive stage of development, the question of power was decided by armed force. Economic changes transferred it to the plane of production itself; it was in this way that the capitalist system came into being. The development of the system later restored war as an essential means in the struggle for power, but under a different form; superiority in the armed struggle presupposes, nowadays, superiority in production itself. If the free play of competition is the final object of production in the hands of the capitalists, its final object in the hands of technicians organized into a State bureaucracy would necessarily be preparation for war. Besides, as Rousseau had already understood, no system of oppression is interested in the welfare of the oppressed; it is on their miserable condition that oppression can rest the more easily the whole of its weight.

As for the moral atmosphere that a régime of bureaucratic dictatorship can bring about, we can realize here and now what it can be like. Capitalism is only a system for exploiting productive work; if we leave out the proletariat's efforts at emancipation, it has given full scope, in every branch of activity, to initiative, free enquiry, invention and genius. On the other hand, the bureaucratic machine, which excludes all judgment and all genius, tends, by its very structure, to concentrate all powers in itself. It therefore threatens the very existence of everything that still remains precious for us in the bourgeois régime.

Instead of the clash of contrary opinions, we should have, on all subjects, an official opinion from which no one would be able to deviate; instead of the cynicism characteristic of the capitalist system, which severs all bonds between man and man in order to replace them by mere relationships of interest, a carefully cultivated fanaticism, calculated to make poverty, in the eyes of the masses, no longer a burden passively to be borne, but a sacrifice freely consented to; a mixture of mystical devotion and unbridled bestiality; a State religion that would stifle all individual values, that is to say all real values. The capitalist system, and even the feudal system, which, through the disorder which it involved, allowed here and there individuals and collectivities to develop in an independent manner, not to mention that blissful Greek system under which the slaves were at least employed in seeing to the wants of free men—all these forms of oppression appear as forms of a free and happy existence when compared with a system that would methodically destroy all initiative, all culture, all thought.

Are we really threatened with subjection to such a system? We are perhaps more than threatened with it; it seems as though we could see it taking shape before our eyes. War, which perpetuates itself under the form of preparation for war, has once and for all given the State an important role in production. Despite the fact that, even in the very heat of the struggle, the capitalists' interests have often come before those of national defence—as the example of Briey shows—systematic preparation for war presupposes in the case of each State a certain regimentation of the economy, a certain tendency towards economic independence. On the other hand, in all spheres, bureaucracy has, since the war, increased in monstrous fashion. Certainly, bureaucracy has not yet turned itself into a system of oppression; if it has crept in everywhere, it nevertheless remains diffused, scattered about in a host of administrative organs which the free play itself of the capitalist system prevents from crystallizing around some central nucleus. Fried, the principal theorist of the review *Die Tat*, said in 1930: "We are practically speaking under the domination of the trade-union bureaucracy, the industrial bureaucracy and the State bureaucracy, and these three bureaucracies are so alike that any one of them could be put in place of another." Now, under the influence of the crisis, these three bureaucracies are tending to merge into one single organization. It is what we see in America, where Roosevelt, under the influence of a band of technicians, is trying to fix prices and wages in agreement with the industrialists' associations and the trade unions. It is what we see in Germany, where, with lightning rapidity, the State apparatus has taken over the trade-union apparatus and is tending to lay its hands on the economy. As for Russia, the three bureaucracies—State, capital industries and workers' organizations—have long since constituted one and the same apparatus.

The question of the prospects lying ahead thus presents itself in two ways. On the one hand, in the case of Russia, where the working masses have expropriated owners and capitalists, the question is whether, without a civil war, the bureaucracy can wipe out the last vestiges of the conquests of October. It certainly seems as though we are compelled by the facts, in spite of Trotsky, to reply in the affirmative. As for other countries, we must consider whether in them capitalism as such can be destroyed without a similar expropriation, through a simple transformation in the meaning of property. On this point, the facts are far less clear. One can certainly say that already the capitalist system, strictly speaking, no longer exists. There is no longer, strictly speaking, a labour market. Regulation of wages and of engagement of labour, the labour corps, seem to be so many steps in the transformation of the wage-earning system into a new form of exploitation. It seems also that in Germany the commissioners placed by Hitler in the trusts and the big undertakings do, in fact, exercise dictatorial powers. The systematic abandonment of gold currency throughout the world is also an important phenomenon. Furthermore, we must bear in mind such facts as the "conclusion of the national revolution" in Germany and the setting up of a supreme economic council which includes all the industrial magnates. Nevertheless, the national-socialist movement is far from having shot its last bolt. The successive acts of surrender made by the bourgeoisie to this movement show well enough what the true relationship between the forces is. The way ownership and industrial management have become separated, which has transformed the majority of owners of capital into mere parasites, permits the use of slogans such as "the struggle against the servitude of interest", which are anti-capitalist without being proletarian. As for the big industrial and financial magnates, their participation in the economic dictatorship of the State does not necessarily exclude the suppression of the part hitherto played by them in the economy. Finally, if political factors may be taken as signs of economic evolution, one cannot disregard the fact that all the political currents which now affect the masses, whether they style themselves fascist, socialist or communist, tend towards the same form of State capitalism. Only a few defenders of economic liberalism oppose this powerful tendency, but they become more and more timid and are less and less listened to. Few indeed are those among our comrades who remember that the workers' democracy could also be set against it. With all these facts, and many others before us, we are obliged to ask ourselves frankly towards what kind of system the present crisis will lead us, if it continues, or, in the event of a rapid return to a favourable situation, the crises to come.

In face of a development of this kind, the worst lapse would be for ourselves to forget the goal we are aiming at. Already a great number of our comrades are more or less seriously infected by this lapse, and it threatens us all. Let us not forget that we want to make the individual, and not the collectivity, the supreme value. We want to form whole men by doing away with that specialization which cripples us all. We want to give to manual labour that dignity which belongs to it of right, by giving the workman the full understanding of technical processes instead of a mere mechanical training; and to provide the understanding with its proper object, by placing it in contact with the world through the medium of labour. We want to make abundantly clear the true relationships between man and nature—those relationships that are concealed, in every society based on exploitation, by "the degrading division of labour into intellectual and manual labour". We want to give back to man, that is to say to the individual, the power which it is his proper function to exercise over nature, over tools, over society itself; to re-establish the importance of the workers as compared with material conditions of work; and, instead of doing away with private property, "to turn individual property into something real, by transforming the means of production . . . which at present serve above all to enslave and exploit labour, into mere instruments of labour freely and co-operatively performed".

That is the proper task of our generation. For several centuries now, ever since the Renaissance, men of thought and men of action have laboured methodically to give the human mind mastery over the forces of nature; and their success has surpassed all expectations. But during the last century it came to be realized that society itself is a force of nature, as blind as the others, as dangerous for man if he does not succeed in mastering it. At the present time this force weighs upon us more cruelly than water, earth, air and fire; all the more so since it holds in its own grasp, as a result of technical progress, the control of water, earth, air and fire. The individual has found himself brutally deprived of the means of combat and of labour; neither war nor production is any longer possible without a total subordination of the individual to the collective industrial machine. Now the social mechanism, through its blind functioning, is in process—as everying that has happened since August 1914 shows—of destroying all the conditions for the material and moral well-being of the individual, all the conditions for intellectual and cultural development. To gain mastery over this mechanism is for us a matter of life and death; and to gain mastery over it means to subject it to the human mind, that is to the individual. In the subordination of society to the individual lies the definition of true democracy and that of socialism as well. But how are we to master this blind force, when it possesses, as Marx has shown in striking phrases, all the intellectual and moral forces crystallized in one monstrous machine? We should look in vain in Marxist literature for a reply to this question.

Are we, then, to despair? Certainly, we would not lack reasons for doing so. It is difficult to see wherein one could place one's hopes. The ability to judge freely is becoming rarer and rarer, more especially in intellectual circles, owing to that specialization which forces each one of us, in the fundamental questions raised by each theoretical piece of research, to believe without understanding. Thus, even in the domain of pure theory, individual judgment finds itself invalidated in face of the results arrived at by collective effort. As for the working class, its position as a passive instrument of production hardly prepares it for taking its own destiny into its hands. The present generations were first of all decimated and demoralized by the war; then peace and prosperity, once restored, brought with them on the one hand a display of wealth and a fever for speculation which have deeply corrupted all classes of the population, and on the other hand technical changes which have deprived the working class of its main strength. For the hope of the revolutionary movement rested on the skilled workmen, the only ones who combined thought and action in industrial work, or who took an active and vital part in the carrying on of the undertaking; the only ones capable of feeling themselves ready to take over one day the responsibility for the whole of economic and political life. Indeed, they formed the most solid nucleus of the revolutionary organizations. And now rationalization has done away with their function and has barely left more than specialized unskilled workmen, completely enslaved to the machine. Then came unemployment, which descended upon the working class thus crippled without producing any reaction. If it has exterminated fewer men than did the war, it has brought about a far more profound demoralization, by reducing great masses of workers, and in particular the whole of the younger generation, to a parasitic condition which, through being prolonged, has come in the end to seem permanent to those who are its victims. The workers who have remained in the factories have at length come themselves to consider the work they do, no longer as an activity indispensible to production, but as a favour granted them by the undertaking. Thus unemployment, where it is most widespread, ends up by reducing the proletariat as a whole to a parasitic frame of mind. It is true that prosperity may return, but no prosperity can now save those generations that have spent their adolescence and youth in a state of idleness more exhausting than work itself, or preserve the coming generations from another crisis or another war.

Can the workers' organizations give the proletariat the strength it lacks? The very complexity of the capitalist system, and consequently of the problems that the struggle to be waged against it raises, carries into the very heart of the working-class movement "the degrading division of labour into manual and intellectual labour". Spontaneous struggle has always proved itself to be ineffective, and organized action almost automatically secretes an administrative apparatus which, sooner or later, becomes oppressive. Nowadays, such oppression is accomplished in the form of an organic liaison either with the national State apparatus or with the Russian State apparatus. Consequently, our efforts run the risk not only of remaining ineffectual, but also of turning themselves against us, to the advantage of our arch-enemy, fascism. The work of agitation, by fanning revolt to white heat, can serve the cause of fascist demagogy, as the example of the German communist party shows. The work of organization, by fostering bureaucracy, can also promote the advent of fascism, as the example of social-democracy shows. Militants cannot take the place of the working class. The emancipation of the workers will be carried out by the workers themselves, or it will not take place at all. Now the most tragic fact of the present time is that the industrial crisis affects the proletariat more profoundly than it does the capitalist class, so that it seems to be not merely the crisis of a system, but of our society itself.

These views will no doubt be taxed with defeatism, even by comrades who endeavour to see clearly. It is doubtful, however, whether we gain anything by using in our ranks the vocabulary of the general staff. With us the very word discouragement ought to have no meaning. The only question that arises is whether we should or should not continue the struggle; if the former, then we shall struggle with as much enthusiasm as if victory were assured. There is no difficulty whatever, once one has decided to act, in maintaining intact, on the level of action, those very hopes which a critical examination has shown to be wellnigh unfounded; in that lies the very essence of courage. Now, seeing that a defeat would run the risk of destroying, for an indefinite period, everything which lends value to human life in our eyes, it is obvious that we must struggle by every means which seems to us to have some chance of proving effective. A man who is thrown overboard in the middle of the ocean ought not to let himself drown, even though there is very little chance of his reaching safety, but to go on swimming until exhausted. And we are not really without hope. The mere fact that we exist, that we conceive and want something different from what exists, constitutes for us a reason for hoping. The working class still contains, scattered here and there, to a large extent outside organized labour, an élite of workers, inspired by that force of mind and spirit that is found only among the proletariat, ready, if need be, to devote themselves wholeheartedly, with the resolution and conscientiousness that a good workman puts into his work, to the building of a rational society. If circumstances are propitious, a spontaneous movement of the masses can carry them to the front of the stage of history. In the meantime, one can only help them to prepare themselves, to think things out, to acquire influence in the workers' organizations that still remain living, that is to say, in the case of France, in the unions, and lastly to band together for the purpose of carrying out, in the streets or in the factories, such actions as are still possible in spite of the present apathy of the masses. An effort tending towards the grouping together of all that has remained healthy at the very heart of industrial undertakings, avoiding both the stirring up of primitive feelings of revolt and the crystallization of an administrative apparatus, may not be much, but there is nothing else. The only hope of socialism resides in those who have already brought about in themselves, as far as is possible in the society of today, that union between manual and intellectual labour which characterizes the society we are aiming at.

But, in addition to this task, the extreme inadequacy of the arms we have at our disposal compels us to undertake another. If, as is only too possible, we are to perish, let us see to it that we do not perish without having existed. The powerful forces that we have to fight are preparing to crush us; and it is true that they can prevent us from existing fully, that is to say from stamping the world with the seal of our will. But there is one sphere in which they are powerless. They cannot stop us from working towards a clear comprehension of the object of our efforts, so that, if we cannot accomplish that which we will, we may at least have willed it, and not just have blindly wished for it; and, on the other hand, our weakness may indeed prevent us from winning, but not from comprehending the force by which we are crushed. Nothing in the world can prevent us from thinking clearly.

There is no contradiction whatever between this task of theoretical elucidation and the tasks set by the actual struggle; on the contrary, there is a correlation, since one cannot act without knowing what one intends and what obstacles have to be overcome. Nevertheless, since the time at our disposal is in any case limited, we are forced to divide it between thought and action, or, to talk more modestly, preparation for action. It is not by any set rule that this division can be determined, but only by the temperament, turn of mind and natural gifts of each one, by the conjectures each one forms about the future, by the chance play of circumstances. At all events, the greatest calamity that could befall us would be to perish incapable both of winning and of understanding.

(*Revolution prolétarienne*, No.158, 25th August, 1933.)

REFLECTIONS CONCERNING TECHNOCRACY, NATIONAL-SOCIALISM, THE U.S.S.R. AND CERTAIN OTHER MATTERS

Here are a few ideas, adventurous perhaps, certainly heretical, as compared with all the accepted orthodoxies, designed above all to make militants think.

We are living on a doctrine elaborated by a great man certainly, but a great man who died fifty years ago. He created a method; he applied it to the phenomena of his time; he could not apply it to the phenomena of our own time.

Pre-war militants felt the need to apply the Marxist method to the new form capitalism had assumed in their day. Lenin's slender brochure on imperialism points to such a concern, for which the day-to-day preoccupations of militants left unfortunately little leisure.

As for ourselves, Marx represents for us, at best, a doctrine; far more often just a name that one hurls at the head of an opponent to pulverize him; almost never a method. Marxism cannot, however, remain something living except as a method of analysis, of which each generation makes use to define the essential phenomena of its own period. Now, it seems that our bodies alone are living in this prodigiously new period, which belies all previous forecasts, and that our minds continue to move, if not at the time of the first International, at any rate in the pre-war period, at the time of the revolutionary C.G.T.[1] and the Russian Bolshevik party. No one tries to define the present period. Trotsky has certainly said, and even repeated on several occasions, that, since 1914, capitalism has entered upon a new phase, that of its decline; but he has never found the time to say what he means by that exactly, nor on what he bases his assertion. One cannot reproach him for this, but it takes away all value from his statement. And no one, so far as I know, has gone any further.

Whoever accepts Lenin's formula, "Without a revolutionary theory there is no revolutionary movement", is compelled to accept also the fact that there is practically no revolutionary movement at the present time.

A little over two years ago a book which caused quite a stir came out in Germany, called *The End of Capitalism*; the author, Ferdinand Fried, belonged to that well-known review, *Die Tat*, which has for a long time advocated a State capitalism, a managed and closed economy, with a dictatorship resting on the twin supports of the trade unions and the national-socialist movement. Revolutionaries have scarcely paid any attention to Fried's book, and have judged it to be second-rate; this is because they have mistakenly sought a coherent system in it, and the value of the book, considered simply as a document, has escaped them. The fundamental idea of the book is the power of the bureaucracy. It is no longer the possessors of the capital, the owners of the plant, who run a business; thanks to shareholding, such owners are very many, and the few big shareholders who control them are concerned above all with financial deals. Those who actually run the business—directors, engineers, technicians of every kind—are, with a few exceptions, not owners but salaried personnel; it is a bureaucracy. At the same time the power of the State, in all countries, has become more and more concentrated in the hands of a bureaucratic machine. Finally, the

[1] Confédération Générale du Travail.

working-class movement is in the hands of a trade-union bureaucracy. "Nowadays we are practically speaking under the domination of the trade-union bureaucracy, the industrial bureaucracy and the State bureaucracy, and these three bureaucracies are so alike that any one of them could be put in place of another." The conclusion is that one must organize a closed economy, managed by this triple bureaucracy united in one and the same machine. This is the very programme of fascism, with this difference, that fascism breaks up the trade-union machinery and creates trade unions placed directly under its control.

There has been a lot of talk in America recently about a new theory called "technocracy". The idea, as the name itself suggests, was that of a new type of economy, which would no longer fluctuate at the mercy of competition, nor be—as socialism wants it to be—in the hands of the workers either, but would be managed by technicians invested with a sort of dictatorial power. The conditions of this new economy, the system of distribution, the currency based on the "unit of energy"—all these are but details. The essential thing was this idea, which has, so we are told, occupied the attention of all Americans for some time, of replacing the capitalist class by another ruling class, which would have been none other than that very industrial bureaucracy Fried refers to.

These absolutely new currents of thought, which are characteristic of the post-war period, and have developed with the present industrial crisis, should lead us to examine what has become nowadays of the process of industrial production. And we must recognize that the two economic categories established by Marx—capitalists and proletariat— are no longer sufficient to grasp the form of production. The capitalists have detached themselves more and more from production itself in order to devote themselves to economic warfare. The first oil king, Rockefeller, achieved his supremacy through a happy idea of an industrial description—the pipe-line; the second, Deterding, only became Rockefeller's lucky rival thanks to deals on the Stock Exchange and financial manipulations. This order of succession is symbolic.

Whether as a caste or as a class, bureaucracy is a new factor in the social struggle. In the U.S.S.R., it has transformed the dictatorship of the proletariat into a dictatorship exercised by itself, and has since directed the revolutionary workers of the entire world. In Germany, on the other hand, it has allied itself with financial capital to exterminate the best of the workers. One can say that in neither case has it played an independent role; but, as long as feudalism lasted, the bourgeoisie, too, had to ally themselves with the oppressed classes against it, or with it against the oppressed classes. What is serious is that nowhere are the workers organized in an independent manner. The communists obey this Russian bureaucracy, just as incapable at the moment of playing a progressive part in the rest of the world as was the French bourgeoisie after Thermidor, when it had crushed those *sans-culottes* on whom it had relied for support. The "reformist" workers are in the hands of that trade-union bureaucracy which resembles the industrial and State bureaucracies as one drop of water does two other drops, and adheres mechanically to the State machine. The anarchists escape the bureaucratic hold only because they know nothing about action methodically organized. Faced with this situation, the controversial utterances of the oppositional communists, the revolutionary trade unionists, etc., seem at any rate to be singularly lacking in topical interest.

The communists accuse the social-democrats of being the "quartermaster-sergeants of fascism", and they are absolutely right. They boast that they are a party capable of fighting fascism effectively, and they are unfortunately wrong. Confronted with the fascist menace, the one question that concerns militants is this. Is it possible to organize the workers in a given country without such organization secreting as it were a bureaucracy which immediately places the organization under a State machine, whether that of the country itself, or that of the U.S.S.R.?

The sinister comedy which social-democracy and the Communist International[1] have now been playing for so many months at the

---

[1] The most fanatical communists ought to open their eyes before the call sent out by the Communist International on March 5th. For months and months past, the "oppositionals" have been insulted because they proclaimed the urgency of proposals for a single front at the top. At the beginning of February, the German communist party proudly, rejected, without even offering to negotiate, the "pact of non-aggression proposed by the social-democrats. On February 19th, the Socialist International proposed a single front unconditionally, and obtained no other answer than Thorez's speech before the Central Committee against any single front at the top, against any suspension of the attacks directed against the social-democrats. Then came the burning of the Reichstag, the arrest of thousands of militants, the terror which outlawed social-democrats and communists

expense of the German proletariat shows that the question is urgent, and perhaps the only one that matters at the moment.

ON LENIN'S BOOK *MATERIALISM AND EMPIRIOCRITICISM*

This work, the only one published by Lenin on purely philosophical questions, is directed against Mach and against the disciples, avowed or not, whom he had in 1908 in the ranks of social-democracy, and especially Russian social-democracy; the best known of these was Bogdanov. Here Lenin examines in detail his opponents' doctrines, which all endeavoured, with more or less subtlety, to solve the problem of knowledge by doing away with the notion of an object exterior to thought; he shows that they all come back in the end, once stripped of their pretentious phraseology, to the idealism of Berkeley, that is to say to a negation of the outside world; he places in opposition to them the materialism of Marx and Engels. In this controversy, which took him away from his usual preoccupations, Lenin displayed once again his power of work, his taste for serious documentary analysis. The point of the discussion is easy to understand: you cannot claim to stand for "scientific socialism" if you have not a clear idea of what science is, if consequently you have not posited in clear terms the problem of knowledge, of the relationship between thought and its object. Nevertheless, Lenin's work is almost as tedious and even almost as little instructive as any textbook of philosophy. This is partly due to the mediocrity of the opponents Lenin is attacking, but above all to Lenin's method itself.

Lenin studied philosophy first of all in 1899, when he was in Siberia; then in 1908, when he was preparing the book in question

---

alike, and pushed the panic-stricken social-democrat leaders into the arms of Hitler (cf. Well's letter), which made all propaganda and organization work almost impossible. And then, and then only, the Communist international, on March 5th, accepted, not only the proposal of February 19th, but even the "pact of non-aggression"! So there was no principle precluding such tactics? What was then to stop their being adopted in February, or even in January, or even before that, when the German proletariat could still take the offensive and fight with serious chances of success? Does not this delay amount to a betrayal?

with a very definite object, namely, in order to refute the theorists in the working-class movement who wished to deviate from the materialism of Engels. That is a very characteristic method which consists in thinking with the object of refuting, the solution being already given before the research. And by what, then, could this solution be given? By the Party, as it is given for the Catholic by the Church. For "the theory of knowledge, exactly in the same way as political economy, is, in our contemporary society, a party science".

As a matter of fact, one cannot deny that there is a close connection between theoretical culture and the division of society into classes. All oppressive societies give birth to a false conception of the relationship between man and nature, from the mere fact that it is only the downtrodden who are in direct contact with nature, that is to say those who are excluded from theoretical culture, deprived of the right of and opportunity for self-expression; and conversely, the false conception so formed tends to prolong the duration of the oppression, in so far as it causes this separation between thought and work to seem legitimate. In this sense, one is able to say of such and such a philosophical system, of such and such a conception of science, that they are reactionary or bourgeois. But it is not in this way that Lenin seems to understand it. He does not say: such and such a conception distorts the true relationship between man and the world, therefore it is reactionary; but, such and such a conception deviates from materialism, leads to idealism, furnishes religion with arguments; it is reactionary, therefore false. He was not at all concerned with seeing clearly into his own thought, but solely with maintaining intact the philosophical traditions on which the Party lived.

Such a method of thought is not that of a free man. And yet in what other way would Lenin have been able to think? As soon as a party finds itself cemented not only by the co-ordination of activities, but also by unity of doctrine, it becomes impossible for a good militant to think otherwise than in the manner of a slave. It is easy thenceforward to visualize how such a party will behave, once it is in power. The stifling régime which weighs at present upon the Russian people was already implied in embryo in Lenin's attitude towards his own process of thought. Long before it robbed the whole of Russia of liberty of thought, the Bolshevik party had already taken it away from their own leader.

Marx, fortunately, went about the process of thinking in a different way. In spite of a number of controversies which add nothing to his prestige, he sought rather to put some order into his own thoughts than to lay flat his opponents; and he had learnt from Hegel that instead of refuting incomplete notions it is better "to surmount them whilst retaining them". That is why Marx's thought differs sensibly from that of the Marxists, Engels included, and nowhere so much as in the solution of the problem with which Lenin is dealing here, namely, that of knowledge and, more generally, of the relations between the mind and the world.

In order to explain how it happens that the mind has knowledge of the world, one can either visualize the world as being a mere creation of the mind, or visualize the mind as being one of the products of the world—a product which, by an inexplicable coincidence, also constitutes its image or reflection. Lenin submits that every philosophy must come back, in the end, to one or other of these two conceptions, and he chooses, of course, the second. He quotes Engels's formula according to which the mind and consciousness "are products of the human brain, being, in the last resort, products of nature"; so that "the products of the human brain being, in the last resort, products of nature, far from being in contradiction with the general scheme of nature, correspond to it"; and he repeats *ad nauseam* that this correspondence lies in the fact that the products of the human brain are, apparently thanks to Providence, the photographs, images, reflections of nature. As if the thoughts of a madman were not, by the same token, "products of nature"!

Now the two conceptions between which Lenin wants to force us to choose both proceed from the same method; in order to solve the problem, they eliminate one of its terms. One of them eliminates the world, the object of knowledge, the other the mind, the subject of knowledge; each strips knowledge of all meaning. If you want, not to construct a theory, but to ascertain the condition in which man is actually placed, you will not ask yourself how it happens that the world is known, but how, in fact, man knows the world; and you will have to acknowledge the existence both of a world which lies beyond mind and of a mind which, far from passively reflecting the world, exercises itself on the world with the double aim of knowing it and transforming it. This is the way Descartes thought; but it is significant that Lenin, in this book, does not even mention his name; this is also, undoubtedly, the way Marx thought.

It will doubtless be objected that Marx never expressed himself in disagreement with the doctrine expounded by Engels in his philosophical works; that he read *Anti-Dühring* in manuscript and approved it; but this only means that Marx never took the time to think over these problems sufficiently to become aware of what separated him from Engels. The entire works of Marx are permeated with a spirit incompatible with the vulgar materialism of Engels and Lenin. He never regards man as being a mere part of nature, but always as being at the same time, owing to the fact that he exercises a free activity, an antagonistic term *vis-à-vis* nature. In a study on Spinoza, he expressly reproaches him with confounding together man and the nature which contains him, instead of placing them in opposition. In his *Dissertations on Feuerbach*, he writes: "The chief defect in all the materialistic doctrines that have so far been elaborated, including Feuerbach's, lies in the fact that the real, the sensible, are conceived only in the form of object, of contemplation, and not as sensible human activity, as *praxis*, in a subjective way. That is why the active side has been developed—in an abstract way, it is true—in opposition to materialism, by idealism, which, of course, does not know real, sensible activity as such."

Although these pronouncements are obscure, they at least state clearly that it is a question of making a synthesis of idealism and materialism, a synthesis in which a radical opposition between passive nature and human activity is preserved. Actually, Marx refuses to conceive of pure thought exercising itself outside all contact with nature; but there is nothing in common between a doctrine which turns man as a whole into a mere product of nature, mind into a mere reflection, and a conception which shows reality appearing as a result of contact between mind and the world, in the act by which thinking man takes possession of the world.

It is according to this conception that we must interpret historical materialism, which means, as Marx explains at length in his *German Ideology*, that the thoughts formed by men in the midst of given technical, economic and social conditions correspond to the way in which they act upon nature by producing their own conditions of existence. Finally, it is from this conception that the idea itself of the proletarian revolution must be drawn; for the very essence of the capitalist system consists, as Marx forcibly showed, of a "reversal of the relationship between subject and object", a reversal brought about by the subordination of subject to object, of "the worker to the material conditions of work"; and the revolution can have no other meaning except to restore to the thinking subject his proper relationship to matter, by giving him back the control which it is his function to exercise over it.

It is not in the least surprising that the Bolshevik party, whose very organization has always rested on the subordination of the individual, and which, once in power, was to enslave the worker to the machine every bit as much as capitalism, should have adopted as its doctrine the naïve materialism of Engels rather than the philosophy of Marx. Nor is it surprising that Lenin should have kept to a purely polemical method and preferred to entangle his opponents in all sorts of difficulties, rather than show how his materialistic theory would have avoided like difficulties. For him, a quotation from *Anti-Dühring* takes the place of all analyses; but it is not by speaking disdainfully of the "errors, long since refuted, committed by Kant" that he can prevent the *Critique of Pure Reason* from remaining, in spite of its omissions, far more instructive than *Anti-Dühring* for anyone who wishes to ponder the problem of knowledge. And one can only laugh on seeing him—him who has constantly invoked "dialectical materialism" as a complete doctrine, capable of solving everything—admit, in a fragment concerning dialectics, that so far one has only been concerned with popularizing the dialectical method, and not with verifying its truth through the history of the sciences.

Such a work is a very distressing mark of the socialist movement's deficiency in the domain of pure theory. And one cannot console oneself for it by saying that social and political action are more important than philosophy; the revolution has got to be as much an intellectual as a social revolution, and purely theoretical speculation has its part therein, a part which it cannot renounce under pain of making all the rest impossible. All genuine revolutionaries have understood that the revolution implies the dissemination of knowledge among the population as a whole. On that score there is complete agreement between Blanqui, who regards communism as impossible before "enlightenment" has been spread everywhere; Bakunin, who wished to see science, according to his admirable expression, "become fused with the real and immediate life of every individual"; and Marx, for whom socialism was to be, above all, the abolition of the "degrading division of labour into intellectual and manual labour".

However, we do not seem to have understood what the conditions of such a transformation are. To send every citizen to secondary school and university up to the age of 18 or 20 would be a feeble, not to say a useless, remedy for the actual state of things from which we suffer. If it were simply a question of popularizing science such as our scientists have made it for us, it would be an easy matter; but nothing about present-day science can be popularized, unless it be the results, and this compels those one imagines one is instructing to believe without understanding. As for the methods which constitute the very soul of science, these are by their very essence unfathomable to laymen, and consequently also to scientists themselves, whom specialization always turns into laymen outside their own very restricted field of study.

Thus, just in the same way as the worker, in modern industrial production, has to submit to the material conditions of his work, so the mind, in scientific research, has nowadays to submit to established scientific facts; and science, which was to have made all things clear and unveiled all mysteries, has itself become the outstanding mystery, so much so that obscurity, and indeed absurdity, appear today in a scientific theory as a mark of profundity.

Science has become the most modern form of the consciousness of man who has not yet found himself or has once again lost himself, to apply Marx's telling dictum concerning religion. And no doubt present-day science can serve very suitably as a theology for our more and more bureaucracy-ridden society, if it is true, as Marx wrote in his youth, that "the universal soul of bureaucracy is secrecy, mystery, inwardly through its hierarchical system, outwardly through its character of closed corporation". More generally, the condition of all privilege, and consequently of all oppression, is the existence of a corpus of knowledge essentially closed to the working masses, which thus find themselves compelled to believe just in the same way as they are forced to obey. Religion, nowadays, no longer suffices to fill this role, and science has taken its place. That is why Marx's excellent observation about the criticism of religion, as being the condition of all criticism, must be extended also to include modern science. Socialism will not even be conceivable as long as science has not been stripped of its mystery.

Descartes thought, in his time, he had founded a science without mystery, that is to say a science wherein there would be so much unity and simplicity of method that the most complicated parts would merely take longer and not be more difficult to understand than the simplest parts; in which everyone would therefore be able to under-stand how the actual results which he had not the time to verify had been obtained; in which each result would be given with the method leading to its discovery, in such a way that every schoolboy would have the feeling of inventing science anew. It was Descartes, too, who formed the project of a School of Arts and Crafts, where each artisan would learn fully to understand the theoretical bases of his own craft; he thus showed himself to be more socialist, in the matter of culture, than all Marx's disciples have been. However, he only accomplished what he wanted to a very limited extent, and even betrayed himself, out of vanity, by publishing a wilfully obscure *Géométrie*. Since his day, there have been hardly any scientists seeking to undermine their own caste privileges. As for the intellectuals of the working-class movement, they have not thought of tackling such an indispensable task; an overwhelm-ing task, it is true, which implies a critical re-examination of the whole of science, and especially of mathematics, where the quintessence of mystery has taken refuge; but a task clearly set by the very notion of socialism, whose accomplishment, independent of outside conditions and the present position of the working-class movement, depends solely on those who will dare to undertake it; furthermore, of such importance that one step made in this direction would be more useful perhaps to humanity and to the proletariat than a whole host of partial successes in the sphere of action. But the theorists of the socialist movement, when they leave the sphere of practical action or that use-less commotion amidst rival tendencies, groups and sub-groups which gives them the illusion of action, never think at all of undermining the privileges of the intellectual caste—far from it; instead, they elaborate a complicated and mysterious doctrine which serves to maintain bureaucratic oppression at the heart of the working-class movement. In this sense, philosophy is indeed, as Lenin said, a party matter.

(*Critique sociale*, November 1933.)

REFLECTIONS CONCERNING THE CAUSES OF LIBERTY AND SOCIAL OPPRESSION

> With regard to human affairs, not to laugh, not to cry, not to become indignant, but to understand.
>
> Spinoza

> The being gifted with reason can make every obstacle serve as material for his work, and turn it to account.
>
> Marcus Aurelius

The present period is one of those when everything that seems normally to constitute a reason for living dwindles away, when one must, on pain of sinking into confusion or apathy, call everything in question again. That the triumph of authoritarian and nationalist movements should blast almost everywhere the hopes that well-meaning people had placed in democracy and in pacifism is only a part of the evil from which we are suffering; it is far deeper and far more widespread. One may well ask oneself if there exists a single sphere of public or private life where the very spring-heads of activity and of hope have not been poisoned by the conditions under which we live. Work is no longer done with the proud consciousness that one is being useful, but with the humiliating and agonizing feeling of enjoying a privilege bestowed by a temporary stroke of fortune, a privilege from which one excludes several human beings by the mere fact that one enjoys, in short, a job. The leaders of industry themselves have lost that naïve belief in unlimited economic progress which made them imagine that they had a mission. Technical progress seems to have gone bankrupt, since instead of happiness it has only brought the masses that physical and moral wretchedness in which we see them floundering; moreover, technical innovations are now banned everywhere, or very nearly so, except in industries connected with war. As for scientific progress, it is difficult to see what can be the use of piling up still more knowledge on to a heap already much too vast to be able to be embraced by the minds even of specialists; and experience has shown that our fore-fathers were mistaken in believing in the spread of enlightenment, since all that can be revealed to the masses is a miserable caricature of modern scientific culture, a caricature which, far from forming their judgment, accustoms them to be credulous. Art itself suffers the back-lash of the general confusion, which partly deprives it of its public, and by that very fact impairs inspiration. Finally, family life has become nothing but anxiety, now that society is closed to the young. The very generation for whom a feverish expectation of the future is the whole of life, vegetates, all over the world, with the feeling that it has no future, that there is no room for it in our world. But if this evil is felt more sharply by youth, it remains common to the whole of humanity today. We are living through a period bereft of a future. Waiting for that which is to come is no longer a matter of hope, but of anguish.

However, ever since 1789, there has been one magic word which contains within itself all imaginable futures, and is never so full of hope as in desperate situations—that word is revolution. That is why, for some time now, we have often been hearing it uttered. We ought, so it seems, to be in a period of full revolution; but in fact everything goes on as if the revolutionary movement were falling into decay with the very system it aspires to destroy. For more than a century, each new generation of revolutionaries has, in turn, placed its hopes in an impending revolution; today, these hopes have lost everything which was able to serve them as buttresses. Neither in the régime that emerged from the October Revolution, nor in the two Internationals, nor in the independent socialist or communist parties, nor in the trade unions, nor in the anarchist organizations, nor in the small youth groups that have sprung up in such profusion in recent times, can one find anything vigorous, healthy or pure; for a long time now the working class has shown no sign of that spontaneity on which Rosa Luxemburg counted, and which, moreover, has never manifested itself without being promptly drowned in blood; the middle classes are only attracted by revolution when it is conjured up for demagogic purposes by apprentice dictators. It is often said that the situation is objectively revolutionary, and that all that is lacking is the "subjective factor"; as if the complete absence of that very force which alone could transform the system were not an objective characteristic of the present situation, whose origins must be sought in the structure of our society! That is why the first duty the present period imposes on us is to have enough intellectual courage to ask ourselves if the term "revolution" is anything else but a name, if it has any precise content, if it is not simply one of the numerous lies produced by the capitalist system in its rise to power which the present crisis is doing us the service of dissipating. This question seems impious, in view of all the pure and noble human beings who have sacrificed everything, their life included, in the service of this word. But only priests can claim to measure the value of an idea by the amount of blood it has caused to be shed. Who knows whether the revolutionaries have not shed their blood as vainly as those Greeks and Trojans of the poet, who, cheated by a false semblance, fought each other for ten years around the shade of Helen?

CRITIQUE OF MARXISM

Up to now all those who have experienced the need to buttress their revolutionary feelings with precise concepts have found or thought they found these concepts in Marx. It is accepted once and for all that Marx, thanks to his general theory of history and to his analysis of bourgeois society, demonstrated the ineluctable necessity of an early upheaval, in which the oppression we suffer under capitalism would be abolished; and indeed, by dint of being persuaded of the fact, we generally dispense with examining. the demonstration more closely.

"Scientific socialism" has attained the status of a dogma, exactly in the same way as have all the results obtained by modern science, results in which each one thinks it is his duty to believe, without ever dreaming of enquiring into the method employed. As far as Marx is concerned, if one tries really to grasp his demonstration intellectually, one at once perceives that it contains very many more difficulties than the advocates of "scientific socialism" lead one to suppose.

Actually, Marx gives a first-rate account of the mechanism of capitalist oppression; but so good is it that one finds it hard to visualize how this mechanism could cease to function. As a rule, it is only the economic aspect of this oppression that holds our attention, that is to say the extortion of surplus value; and, if we confine ourselves to this point of view, it is certainly easy to explain to the masses that this extortion is bound up with competition, which latter is in turn bound up with private property, and that the day when property becomes collective all will be well. Nevertheless, even within the limits of this apparently simple reasoning, a thousand difficulties present themselves on careful examination. For Marx showed clearly that the true reason for the exploitation of the workers is not any desire on the part of the capitalists to enjoy and consume, but the need to expand the undertaking as rapidly as possible so as to make it more powerful than its rivals. Now not only a business undertaking, but any sort of working collectivity, no matter what it may be, has to exercise the maximum restraint on the consumption of its members so as to devote as much time as possible to forging weapons for use against rival collectivities; so that as long as there is, on the surface of the globe, a struggle for power, and as long as the decisive factor in victory is industrial production, the workers will be exploited. As a matter of fact, what Marx assumed, without, however, proving it, was that every kind of struggle for power will disappear on the day socialism is established in all industrial countries; the only trouble is that, as Marx himself recognized, revolution cannot take place everywhere at once; and when it does take place in one country, it does not for that country do away with the need for exploiting and oppressing the mass of workers, but on the contrary accentuates the need, lest it be found weaker than the other nations. The history of the Russian Revolution furnishes a painful illustration of this.

If we consider other aspects of capitalist oppression, other still more formidable difficulties appear, or rather the same difficulty under a more glaring light. The power which the bourgeoisie has to exploit and oppress the workers lies at the very foundations of our social life, and cannot be destroyed by any political and juridical transformation. This power consists in the first place and essentially in the modern system of production itself, that is to say big industry. Pungent dicta abound in Marx's writings on this subject of living labour being enslaved to dead labour, "the reversal of the relationship between subject and object", "the subordination of the worker to the material conditions of work". "In the factory", he writes in *Capital*, "there exists a mechanism independent of the workers, which incorporates them as living cogs. . . . The separation of the spiritual forces that play a part in production from manual labour, and the transformation of the former into power exercised by capital over labour, attain their fulfilment in big industry founded on mechanization. The detail of the individual destiny of the machine-worker fades into insignificance before the science, the tremendous natural forces and the collective labour which are incorporated in the machines as a whole and constitute with them the employer's power." Thus the worker's complete subordination to the undertaking and to those who run it is founded on the factory organization and not on the system of property. Similarly, "the separation of the spiritual forces that play a part in production from manual labour", or, according to another formula, "the degrading division of labour into manual and intellectual labour", is the very foundation of our culture, which is a culture of specialists. Science is a monopoly, not because public education is badly organized, but by its very nature; non-scientists have access only to the results, not to the methods, that is to say they can only believe, not assimilate. "Scientific socialism" has itself remained the monopoly of a select few, and the "intellectuals" possess, unfortunately, the same privileges in the working-class movement as they do in bourgeois society. And the same applies, furthermore, on the political plane.

Marx had clearly perceived that State oppression is founded on the existence of organs of government that are permanent and distinct from the population, namely, the bureaucratic, military and police machines; but these permanent organs are the inevitable result of the radical distinction existing, in fact, between the managerial and executive functions. In this respect again, the working-class movement reproduces in full the vices of bourgeois society. At all levels we are brought up against the same obstacle. The whole of our civilization is founded on specialization, which implies the enslavement of those who execute to those who co-ordinate; and on such a basis one can only organize and perfect oppression, not lighten it. Far from capitalist society having developed within itself the material conditions for a régime of liberty and equality, the establishment of such a régime presupposes a preliminary transformation in the realm of production and that of culture.

We can only understand how Marx and his disciples could still believe in the possibility of a real democracy based on our present civilization if we take into account their theory of the development of productive forces. It is well known that, in Marx's eyes, this development constitutes, in the last analysis, the true motive power of history, and that it is practically unlimited. Every social system, every dominant class has the "task", the "historic mission", of carrying the productive forces to an ever higher level, until the day when all further progress is arrested by the social cadres; at that moment the productive forces rebel, break up these cadres, and a new class takes over power. The recognition of the fact that the capitalist system grinds down millions of men only enables one to condemn it morally; what constitutes the historic condemnation of the system is the fact that, after having made productive progress possible, it is now an obstacle in its way. The essential task of revolutions consists in the emancipation not of men but of productive forces. As a matter of fact, it is clear that, as soon as these have reached a level of development high enough for production to be carried out at the cost of little effort, the two tasks coincide; and Marx assumed that such was the case in our time. It was this assumption that enabled him to establish a harmony, indispensable to his moral tranquillity, between his idealistic aspirations and his materialistic conception of history. In his view, modern technique, once freed from capitalist forms of economy, can give men, here and now, sufficient leisure to enable them to develop their faculties harmoniously, and consequently bring about the disappearance, to a certain extent, of the degrading specialization created by capitalism; and above all the further development of technique must lighten more and more, day by day, the burden of material necessity, and as an immediate consequence that of social constraint, until humanity reaches at last a truly paradisal state in which the most abundant production would be at the cost of a trifling expenditure of effort and the ancient curse of work would be lifted; in short, in which the happiness of Adam and Eve before the fall would be regained.

One can understand very well, starting from this conception, the attitude of the Bolsheviks, and why all of them, including Trotsky, treat democratic ideas with supreme disdain. They have found themselves powerless to bring about the workers' democracy foreshadowed by Marx; but such a minor detail does not worry them, convinced as they are, on the one hand, that all attempts at social action which do not consist of developing productive forces are doomed to failure, on the other hand, that all progress in productive forces causes humanity to advance along the road leading to emancipation, even if it is at the cost of a temporary oppression. It is not surprising that, backed up by such moral certainty as this, they have astonished the world by their strength.

It is seldom, however, that comforting beliefs are at the same time rational. Before even examining the Marxist conception of productive forces, one is struck by the mythological character it presents in all socialist literature, where it is assumed as a postulate. Marx never explains why productive forces should tend to increase; by accepting without proof this mysterious tendency, he allies himself not with Darwin, as he liked to think, but with Lamarck, who in similar fashion founded his biological system on an inexplicable tendency of living creatures to adapt themselves. In the same way, why is it that, when social institutions are in opposition to the development of productive forces, victory should necessarily belong beforehand to the latter rather than the former? Marx evidently does not assume that men consciously transform their social conditions in order to improve their economic conditions; he knows perfectly well that up to the present social transformations have never been accompanied by any clear realization of their real long-term consequences; he therefore implicitly assumes that productive forces possess a secret virtue enabling them to overcome obstacles. Finally, why does he assert without demonstration, and as a self-evident truth, that the productive forces are capable of unlimited development?

The whole of this doctrine, on which the Marxist conception of revolution entirely rests, is absolutely devoid of any scientific basis. In order to understand it, we must remember the Hegelian origins of Marxist thought. Hegel believed in a hidden mind at work in the universe, and that the history of the world is simply the history of this world mind, which, as in the case of everything spiritual, tends indefinitely towards perfection. Marx claimed to "put back on its feet" the Hegelian dialectic, which he accused of being "upside down", by substituting matter for mind as the motive power of history; but by an extraordinary paradox, he conceived history, starting from this rectification, as though he attributed to matter what is the very essence of mind—an unceasing aspiration towards the best. In this he was profoundly in keeping, moreover, with the general current of capitalist thought; to transfer the principle of progress from mind to things is to give a philosophical expression to that "reversal of the relationship between subject and object" in which Marx discerned the very essence of capitalism. The rise of big industry made of productive forces the divinity of a kind of religion whose influence Marx came under, despite himself, when formulating his conception of history. The term religion may seem surprising in connection with Marx; but to believe that our will coincides with a mysterious will which is at work in the universe and helps us to conquer is to think religiously, to believe in Providence. Besides, Marx's vocabulary itself testifies to this since it contains quasi-mystical expressions such as "the historic mission of the proletariat".

This religion of productive forces, in whose name generations of industrial employers have ground down the labouring masses without the slightest qualm, also constitutes a factor making for oppression within the socialist movement. All religions make man into a mere instrument of Providence, and socialism, too, puts men at the service of historical progress, that is to say of productive progress. That is why, whatever may be the insult inflicted on Marx's memory by the cult which the Russian oppressors of our time entertain for him, it is not altogether undeserved. Marx, it is true, never had any other motive except a generous yearning after liberty and equality; but this yearning, once separated from the materialistic religion with which it was merged in his mind, no longer belongs to anything except what Marx contemptuously called utopian socialism. If Marx's writings contained nothing more valuable than this, they might without loss be forgotten, at any rate except for his economic analyses.

But such is not the case; we find in Marx a different conception from that Hegelian doctrine turned inside out, namely, a materialism which no longer has anything religious about it and forms not a doctrine but a method of understanding and of action. It is no uncommon thing to find thus in quite great minds two distinct and even incompatible conceptions mingling together under cover of the inevitable looseness of language; absorbed as they are in formulating new ideas, such minds have not the time to make a critical examination of what they have discovered. Marx's truly great idea is that in human society as well as in nature nothing takes place otherwise than through material transformations. "Men make their own history, but within certain fixed conditions." To desire is nothing; we have got to know the material conditions which determine our possibilities of action; and in the social sphere these conditions are defined by the way in which man obeys material necessities in supplying his own needs, in other words, by the method of production. A methodical improvement in social organization presupposes a detailed study of the method of production, in order to try to find out on the one hand what we may expect from it, in the immediate or distant future, from the point of view of output, and on the other hand what forms of social and cultural organization are compatible with it, and, finally, how it may itself be transformed. Only irresponsible human beings can neglect such a study and yet claim the right to domineer over society; and, unfortunately, such is the case everywhere, as much in revolutionary circles as among the ruling classes. The materialistic method—that instrument which Marx bequeathed us—is an untried instrument; no Marxist has ever really used it, beginning with Marx himself. The only really valuable idea to be found in Marx's writings is also the only one that has been completely neglected. It is not surprising that the social movements springing from Marx have failed.

The first question to consider is that concerning output. Are there any reasons for supposing that modern technique, at its present level, is capable—always supposing a fair distribution—of guaranteeing to everyone sufficient welfare and leisure so that the development of the individual may cease to be hampered by modern working conditions? It seems that on this subject there are many illusions, purposely kept alive by demagogic interests. It is not profits which have to be calculated; those of them that are reinvested in production would for the most part be taken away from the workers under any system. We should have to be able to calculate the total amount of labour that could be dispensed with at the cost of a transformation of the property system. Even that would not solve the problem; we must bear in mind the labour involved in the complete reorganization of the productive machine, a reorganization necessary for production to be adapted to its new end, namely, the welfare of the masses; we must not forget that the manufacture of armaments would not be abandoned before the capitalist system had been everywhere destroyed; above all, we must provide for the fact that the abolition of individual profit, while causing certain forms of waste to disappear, would at the same time necessarily create others. It is impossible, of course, to make exact calculations; but they are not indispensable for discerning that the abolition of private property would be far from sufficient in itself to prevent work in the mines and in the factories from continuing to weigh as a servitude on those who are subjected to it.

But if the present state of technique is insufficient to liberate the workers, is there at any rate a reasonable hope that an unlimited development lies before it, which would imply an unlimited increase in productivity? This is what everybody assumes, both among capitalists and socialists, without the smallest preliminary study of the question; it is enough that the productivity of human effort should have increased in an unheard of manner for the last three centuries for it to be expected that this increase will continue at the same rate. Our so-called scientific culture has given us this fatal habit of generalizing, of arbitrarily extrapolating, instead of studying the conditions of a given phenomenon and the limits implied by them; and Marx, whose dialectical method should have saved him from such an error, fell into it on this point just like other people.

The problem is fundamental, and of a kind to determine all our future prospects; it must be formulated with the utmost precision. To this end, the first thing is to know in what technical progress consists, what factors play a part in it, and to examine each factor separately; for we mix up under the name of technical progress entirely different procedures that offer different possibilities of development.

The first procedure that offers itself to man for producing more with less effort is the utilization of natural sources of energy; and it is true, in a sense, that it is impossible to assign a precise limit to the benefits of this procedure, because we do not know what new sources of energy we shall one day be able to use; but this does not mean to say that there can be prospects of unlimited progress in this direction, nor that progress in it is, generally speaking, assured. For nature does not give us this energy, whatever may be the form in which it offers itself—animal power, coal or petroleum; we have to wrest it from her and transform it through our labour so as to adapt it to our own ends. Now, this labour does not necessarily become less as time goes on; at present the very opposite is happening to us, since the extraction of coal and petroleum becomes continually and automatically less profitable and more costly. What is more, the deposits at present known are destined to become exhausted at the end of a relatively short time. Perhaps new deposits will be found; but prospecting, the development of new workings, some of which will doubtless fail to pay—all that will be costly; furthermore, we do not know how many unknown deposits there are in general, and in any case their number will not be unlimited. We may also—and no doubt some day we are bound to—discover new sources of energy; but there is nothing to guarantee that their utilization will call for less labour than the utilization of coal or heavy oils; the opposite is just as possible. It may even happen, at the worst, that the utilization of a natural source of energy involves more labour than the human expenditure of energy one is seeking to replace. In this field it is chance which decides; for the discovery of a new and easily accessible source of energy or of an economic transformation process for a known source of energy is not one of those things one is sure of reaching on a basis of thinking methodically and spending the necessary time thereon.

We deceive ourselves in this matter because we are in the habit of considering the development of science from outside and as a whole; we do not realize that if certain scientific results depend entirely on the good use the scientist makes of his reasoning faculties, others are the result of lucky finds. This is so in the case of the utilization of the forces of nature. There is not the least doubt that every source of energy is transformable; but the scientist is no more certain of coming across something economically advantageous in the course of his researches than is the explorer of arriving at a fertile territory. We can find an instructive example of this in the famous experiments connected with the thermic energy of the seas, about which there has been so much— and such useless—excitement. Now, as soon as chance enters in, the idea of continuous progress is no longer applicable. Consequently, to hope that the development of science will one day bring about, in some sort of automatic way, the discovery of a source of energy which would be almost immediately utilizable for all human needs, is simply day-dreaming. One cannot prove that it is impossible; and, strictly speaking, it is possible, too, that one fine day some sudden change in the astronomical order may give to vast expanses of the earth's surface the bewitching climate that enables, so it is said, certain primitive tribes to live without working; but possibilities of this description must never be taken into account. On the whole, it would not be reasonable to try to determine here and now what the future holds in store for the human race in this field.

Apart from this, there exists only one other resource making it possible to diminish the total sum of human effort, namely, what we may call, to use a modern expression, the rationalization of labour. Two aspects of it may be distinguished; one which concerns the relationship between simultaneous efforts, the other that between successive efforts; in both cases progress resides in increasing the productivity of the efforts by the way in which these are combined. It is clear that in this field one can, strictly speaking, leave chance out of account, and that here the notion of progress has a meaning; the question is to know whether this progress is unlimited, and, if not, whether we are still a long way from the limit.

As far as what may be termed the rationalization of labour in space is concerned, the economic factors are the concentration, division and co-ordination of labour. The concentration of labour implies the reduction of all kinds of expenses that may be included all together under the heading of overheads, amongst them those relating to premises, transport, sometimes plant. As for the division of labour, that has far more astonishing results. Sometimes it makes it possible to reach a considerable speed in the execution of work which individual workers by themselves could accomplish as well, but much more slowly, and that because each would have to make on his own account the effort of co-ordination which the organization of labour enables one man to assume on behalf of several others. Adam Smith's famous analysis with regard to the manufacture of pins is an example of this. At other times—and this is what matters most—division and co-ordination of effort make possible gigantic works which would be infinitely beyond the scope of a single man. We must also bear in mind the savings which regional specialization makes possible in the matter of transportation of energy and of raw materials, and doubtless many others besides, which it would take too long to investigate. At all events, as soon as we cast a look at the present system of production, it seems fairly obvious not only that these labour-saving factors contain within themselves a limit beyond which they become factors of expenditure, but furthermore that this limit has been reached and overstepped.

For many years now the expansion of industrial undertakings has been accompanied, not by any reduction in overhead costs, but by an increase in them; the functioning of an undertaking, having become too complex to allow for efficient supervision, leaves an ever wider and wider margin for waste and brings about an accelerated, and no doubt to a certain extent a parasitic, increase in the staff whose task it is to co-ordinate the various branches of the undertaking. The increase in exchange, which formerly played a tremendous role as a factor in economic progress, has begun in its turn to cause more overhead expenses than it avoids, because the goods remain a long time non-productive, because the staff dealing with exchange is itself increasing at an accelerated tempo, and because transport consumes an ever-increasing amount of energy as a result of innovations for increasing speed-innovations that become necessarily more and more costly and less and less efficient as they succeed one another. Thus, in all these respects, progress is transformed nowadays, in a strictly speaking mathematical manner, into regression.

The progress achieved by the co-ordination of effort in time is doubtless the most important factor of technical progress; it is also the

hardest to analyse. Ever since Marx, we have been in the habit of designating it by speaking of the substitution of inanimate labour for living
labour, a dangerously vague formula in the sense that it conjures up the
picture of a continuous evolution towards a stage of technique where,
if one may so express it, all the jobs to be done would be done already.
Such a picture is as chimerical as that of the existence of a natural
source of energy as readily accessible to man as his own vital force. The
substitution in question simply puts in the place of the movements that
would enable certain results to be obtained directly other movements
that produce these results indirectly, thanks to the purposeful
arrangement of inert objects; it still remains a question of entrusting to
matter what seemed to be the role of human effort, but instead of
making use of the energy supplied by certain natural phenomena, use
is made of the resistance, solidity, hardness possessed by certain
materials. In either case, the properties of blind and indifferent matter
can only be adapted to human ends by human labour; and in either
case again, reason forbids one to assume in advance that this work of
adaptation must necessarily be less than the effort that men would have
to make so as to obtain directly the end they have in view. But whereas
the utilization of natural sources of energy depends to a considerable
extent on unforeseeable conjunctures, the utilization of inert and
resistant materials has for the most part been effected according to a
continuous progress which, once one has understood the principle
involved, the mind is capable of embracing and extending.

The first stage—as old as humanity—consists in entrusting to
objects disposed in suitable places all those efforts of resistance whose
aim it is to prevent certain movements on the part of certain things.
The second stage constitutes mechanization as such; mechanization
became possible on the day when it was observed that one could not
only make use of inert matter so as to ensure immobility where this
was necessary, but also entrust it with maintaining the permanent
relationships of movements with one other—relationships which up
to then had on each occasion to be established by the mind. To this
end, all that is necessary is that one should have been able to register
these relationships, suitably transposed, in the forms impressed on
solid matter. It is thus that one of the first developments which made
for the introduction of mechanization consisted in relieving the weaver

of the necessity of adapting the choice of threads to be drawn on his loom to the design of the cloth, and this by means of a piece of cardboard punched with holes corresponding to the design. If transpositions of this nature in the various branches of labour could only be obtained little by little, and thanks to inventions apparently due to inspiration or chance, it is because manual work combines the permanent elements that compose it in such a way as to conceal them more often than not under an appearance of variety; that is why sectionalized hand-fabrication had to precede big industry.

Finally, the third and last stage corresponds to automation, which is only beginning to make its appearance; the principle behind it lies in the possibility of entrusting the machine not only with an operation that is invariably the same, but also with a combination of varied operations. This combination can be as vast, as complex as you like; it is only necessary that the variety of operations should be defined and limited beforehand. Automation, which is still, so to say, at a primitive stage of development, can thus, theoretically, develop indefinitely; and the use of such a technique for satisfying human needs knows no limits save those imposed by the share of the unforeseen in the conditions of human existence. If it were possible to conceive of conditions of existence absolutely devoid of any unforeseen contingency, then the American myth of the robot would have a meaning, and the complete abolition of human labour through a systematic organization of the world would be feasible. It is not so, and these are only fictions; though it would still be useful to formulate these fictions, as an ideal limit, if men had at least the power to reduce progressively by some method or other the share of the unforeseen in their lives. But such is not the case, either, and no technique will ever relieve men of the necessity of continually adapting, by the sweat of their brow, the mechanical equipment they use.

Under these conditions it is easy to conceive that a certain degree of automation might be more costly in human effort than a less advanced degree. At least it is easy to conceive it in an abstract way; it is almost impossible to reach any concrete notion in this matter on account of the great number of factors which would have to be taken into account. The extraction of the metals from which machines are made can be done only with human labour; and as it is a question of mining, the work becomes more and more arduous as it proceeds, not to mention the fact that the known deposits run the risk of becoming exhausted relatively quickly; men reproduce themselves, iron does not. Nor must we forget, though financial balance-sheets, statistics, the publications of economists disdain to note it, that work in the mines is more painful, more exhausting, more dangerous than most other forms of work; iron, coal, potassium—all these products are stained with blood. Besides, automatic machines are only a paying proposition as long as they are used for mass production in enormous quantities; their functioning is therefore bound up with the chaos and waste involved in an excessive economic centralization; furthermore, they create the temptation to produce far more than is required to satisfy real needs, which leads to the squandering of precious stores of human energy and of raw materials. Nor must we leave out of account the expenditure involved in all technical progress, on account of the preliminary research required, the need for adapting other branches of production to this progress, the scrapping of old plant which is often discarded when it could still have served for a long time. Nothing of all this is capable of being even approximately measured. It is only clear, in a general way, that the higher the level of technical efficiency the more the advantages to be derived from new developments diminish as compared with the drawbacks. We have, however, no means of ascertaining exactly whether we are near or far from the limit beyond which technical progress must transform itself into a factor of economic regression. We can only try to guess at it empirically, according to the way in which our contemporary economy is evolving.

Now, what we see is that for some years past, in almost all industries, the various concerns have refused systematically to welcome technical innovations. The socialist and communist press takes advantage of this fact to pour out eloquent diatribes against capitalism, but it omits to explain by what miracle innovations that are at present costly would become economically paying under a socialist system or one so called. It is more reasonable to suppose that in this sphere we are not far from reaching the limit of useful progress; and, seeing that the present-day complexity of economic relations and the formidable extension of credit prevent industrial leaders from immediately perceiving that a once paying factor has ceased to be so, we may even conclude, with all suitable reservations regarding so intricate a problem, that it is very likely this limit has already been overstepped.

A serious study of the question ought, strictly speaking, to take many other elements into consideration. The various factors that go to increase productivity do not develop separately, although they have to be separated in analysis; they combine together, and these combinations produce results difficult to foresee. Besides, technical progress does not only serve to obtain at low cost what one used to obtain before with considerable effort; it also makes it possible to undertake what without it would have been almost unimaginable. It would be as well to examine the value of these new possibilities, while bearing in mind the fact that they are not only possibilities of construction, but also of destruction. But such a study would be forced to take into account the economic and social relations which necessarily go hand in hand with a given form of technical achievement. For the moment it is enough to have understood that the possibility of future progress so far as concerns productivity is not beyond question; that, to all appearances, we have at present as many reasons for expecting to see it diminish as increase; and, what is most important of all, that a continuous and unlimited increase in productivity is, strictly speaking, inconceivable. It is solely the frenzy produced by the speed of technical progress that has brought about the mad idea that work might one day become unnecessary. On the plane of pure science, this idea has found expression in the search for the "perpetual motion machine", that is to say a machine which would go on producing work indefinitely without ever consuming any; and the scientists made short work of it by propounding the law of the conservation of energy. In the social sphere, divagations are better received. The "higher stage of communism", regarded by Marx as the final term of social evolution, is, in effect, a utopia absolutely analogous to that of perpetual motion.

It is in the name of this utopia that revolutionaries have shed their blood. Or rather, they have shed their blood in the name either of this utopia or of the equally utopian belief that the present system of production could be placed by a mere decree at the service of a society of free and equal men. Is it surprising, then, if all this blood has been shed in vain? The history of the working-class movement is thus lit up with a cruel, but singularly vivid, light. The whole of it can be summarized by remarking that the working class has never manifested strength save in so far as it has served something other than the workers' revolution. The working-class movement was able to give the illusion of power as long as it was still a question for it of helping to liquidate the vestiges of feudalism or to prepare the way for capitalist domination, whether under the form of private capitalism or that of State capitalism, as happened in Russia; now that its role in that field is over and the industrial crisis confronts it with the problem of the effective seizure of power by the working masses, it is crumbling away and dissolving with a rapidity that breaks the hearts of those who had placed their faith in it. On its ruins interminable arguments are held which can only be smoothed over by the most ambiguous formulas; for among all those who still persist in talking about revolution, there are perhaps not two who attach the same content to the term. And that is not in the least surprising. The word "revolution" is a word for which you kill, for which you die, for which you send the labouring masses to their death, but which does not possess any content.

Yet perhaps one can give a meaning to the revolutionary ideal, if not as a possible prospect in view, at any rate as a theoretical limit of feasible social transformations. What we should ask of the revolution is the abolition of social oppression; but for this notion to have at least a chance of possessing some meaning, we must be careful to distinguish between oppression and subordination of personal whims to a social order. So long as such a thing as a society exists, it will circumscribe the life of individuals within quite narrow limits and impose its rules on them; but this inevitable constraint does not merit the name of oppression except in so far as, owing to the fact that it brings about a division between those who exercise it and those who are subject to it, it places the latter at the disposal of the former and thus causes those who command to exert a crushing physical and moral pressure over those who execute. Even when this distinction has been made, nothing entitles us to assume a priori that the abolition of oppression is either possible or even simply conceivable by way of limit. Marx demonstrated forcibly, in the course of analyses of whose far-reaching scope he was himself unaware, that the present system of production, namely, big industry, reduces the worker to the position of a wheel in the factory and a mere instrument in the hands of his employers; and it is useless to hope that technical progress will, through a progressive and continuous reduction in productive effort, alleviate, to the point of almost causing it to disappear, the double burden imposed on man by nature and society.

The problem is, therefore, quite clear; it is a question of knowing whether it is possible to conceive of an organization of production which, though powerless to remove the necessities imposed by nature and the social constraint arising therefrom, would enable these at any rate to be exercised without grinding down souls and bodies under oppression. At a time like ours, to have grasped this problem clearly is perhaps a condition for being able to live at peace with oneself. If we can manage to conceive in concrete terms the conditions of this liberating organization, then it only remains for us to exercise, in order to move towards it, all the powers of action, small or great, at our disposal; and if, on the other hand, we realize clearly that the possibility of such a system of production is not even conceivable, we at least gain the advantage of being able legitimately to resign ourselves to oppression and of ceasing to regard ourselves as accomplices in it because we fail to do anything effective to prevent it.

ANALYSIS OF OPPRESSION

The problem is, in short, to know what it is that links oppression in general and each form of oppression in particular to the system of production; in other words, to succeed in grasping the mechanism of oppression, in understanding by what means it arises, subsists, transforms itself, by what means, perhaps, it might theoretically disappear. This is, to all intents and purposes, a novel question. For centuries past, noble minds have regarded the power of oppressors as constituting a usurpation pure and simple, which one had to try to oppose either by simply expressing a radical disapproval of it, or else by armed force placed at the service of justice. In either case, failure has always been complete; and never was it more strikingly so than when it took on momentarily the appearance of victory, as happened with the French Revolution, when, after having effectively succeeded in bringing about the disappearance of a certain form of oppression, people stood by, helpless, watching a new oppression immediately being set up in its place.

In his ponderings over this resounding failure, which had come to crown all previous ones, Marx finally came to understand that you cannot abolish oppression so long as the causes which make it inevitable remain, and that these causes reside in the objective—that is to say material—conditions of the social system. He consequently elaborated a completely new conception of oppression, no longer considered as the usurpation of a privilege, but as the organ of a social function. This function is that very one which consists in developing the productive forces, in so far as this development calls for severe efforts and serious hardships; and Marx and Engels perceived a reciprocal relationship between this development and social oppression.

In the first place, according to them, oppression becomes established only when improvements in production have brought about a division of labour sufficiently advanced for exchange, military command and government to constitute distinct functions; on the other hand, oppression, once established, stimulates the further development of the productive forces, and changes in form as and when this development so demands, until the day when, having become a hindrance to it instead of a help, it disappears purely and simply.

However brilliant the concrete analyses may be by which Marxists have illustrated this thesis, and although it constitutes an improvement on the naïve expressions of indignation which it replaced, one cannot say that it throws light on the mechanism of oppression. It only partially describes its origins; for why should the division of labour necessarily turn into oppression? It by no means entitles us to a reasonable expectation of its ending; for if Marx believed himself to have shown how the capitalist system finally hinders production, he did not even attempt to prove that, in our day, any other oppressive system would hinder it in like manner. Furthermore, one fails to understand why oppression should not manage to continue, even after it has become a factor of economic regression. Above all, Marx omits to explain why oppression is invincible as long as it is useful, why the oppressed in revolt have never succeeded in founding a non-oppressive society, whether on the basis of the productive forces of their time, or even at the cost of an economic regression which could hardly increase their misery; and, lastly, he leaves completely in the dark the general principles of the mechanism by which a given form of oppression is replaced by another.

What is more, not only have Marxists not solved a single one of these problems, but they have not even thought it their duty to formulate them. It has seemed to them that they had sufficiently accounted for social oppression by assuming that it corresponds to a function in the struggle against nature. Even then, they have only really brought out this correspondence in the case of the capitalist system; but, in any case, to suppose that such a correspondence constitutes an explanation of the phenomenon is to apply unconsciously to social organisms Lamarck's famous principle, as unintelligible as it is convenient, "the function creates the organ". Biology only started to be a science on the day when Darwin replaced this principle by the notion of conditions of existence. The improvement lies in the fact that the function is no longer considered as the cause, but as the result of the organ—the only intelligible order; the part played by cause is henceforth attributed only to a blind mechanism, that of heredity combined with accidental variations. Actually, by itself, all this blind mechanism can do is to produce haphazardly anything whatsoever; the adaptation of the organ to the function here enters into play in such a manner as to limit chance by eliminating the non-viable structures, no longer as a mysterious tendency, but as a condition of existence; and this condition is defined by the relationship of the organism under consideration to its partly inert, partly living environment, and more especially to similar rival organisms. Adaptation is henceforth conceived in regard to living beings as an exterior and no longer an interior necessity.

It is clear that this luminous method is not only valid in biology, but wherever one is confronted by organized structures which have not been organized by anybody. In order to be able to appeal to science in social matters, we ought to have effected with respect to Marxism an improvement similar to that which Darwin effected with respect to Lamarck. The causes of social evolution must no longer be sought elsewhere than in the daily efforts of men considered as individuals. These efforts are certainly not directed haphazardly; they depend, in each individual case, on temperament, education, routine, customs, prejudices, natural or acquired needs, environment, and above all, broadly speaking, human nature, a term which, although difficult to define, is probably not devoid of meaning. But given the almost infinite diversity of individuals, and especially the fact that human nature includes among other things the ability to innovate, to create, to rise above oneself, this warp and woof of incoherent efforts would produce anything whatever in the way of social organization, were it not that chance found itself restricted in this field by the conditions of existence to which every society has to conform on pain of being either subdued or destroyed. The men who submit to these conditions of existence are more often than not unaware of them, for they act not by imposing a definite direction on the efforts of each one, but by rendering ineffective all efforts made in directions disallowed by them.

These conditions of existence are determined in the first place, as in the case of living beings, on the one hand by the natural environment and on the other hand by the existence, activity and especially competition of other organisms of the same species, that is to say here of other social groups. But still a third factor enters into play, namely, the organization of the natural environment, capital equipment, armaments, methods of work and of warfare; and this factor occupies a special position owing to the fact that, though it acts upon the form of social organization, it in turn undergoes the latter's reaction upon it. Furthermore, this factor is the only one over which the members of a society can perhaps exercise some control.

This outline is too abstract to serve as a guide; but if on the basis of this summary view we could arrive at some concrete analyses, it would at last become possible to formulate the social problem. The enlightened goodwill of men acting in an individual capacity is the only possible principle of social progress; if social necessities, once clearly perceived, were found to lie outside the range of this goodwill in the same way as those which govern the stars, each man would have nothing more to do but to watch history unfolding as one watches the seasons go by, while doing his best to spare himself and his loved ones the misfortune of being either an instrument or a victim of social oppression. If this is not so, it would be necessary first of all to define by way of an ideal limit the objective conditions that would permit of a social organization absolutely free from oppression; then seek out by what means and to what extent the conditions actually given can be

transformed so as to bring them nearer to this ideal; find out what is
the least oppressive form of social organization for a body of specific
objective conditions; and lastly, define in this field the power of action
and responsibilities of individuals as such. Only on this condition
could political action become something analogous to a form of work,
instead of being, as has been the case hitherto, either a game or a
branch of magic.

Unfortunately, in order to reach this stage, what is required is not
only searching, rigorous thinking, subjected, so as to avoid all possibility of error, to the most exacting checking, but also historical, technical
and scientific investigations of an unparalleled range and precision, and
conducted from an entirely new point of view. However, events do not
wait; time will not stop in order to afford us leisure; the present forces
itself urgently on our attention and threatens us with calamities which
would bring in their train, amongst many other harrowing mis-
fortunes, the material impossibility of studying or writing otherwise
than in the service of the oppressors. What are we to do? There would
be no point in letting oneself be swept along in the *mêlée* by an ill-
considered enthusiasm. No one has the faintest idea of either the
objectives or the means of what is still from force of habit called
revolutionary action. As for reformism, the principle of the lesser evil
on which it is based is certainly eminently reasonable, however discredited it may be through the fault of those who have hitherto made
use of it; though remember, if it has so far served only as a pretext for
capitulation, this is due not to the cowardice of a few leaders, but to an
ignorance unfortunately common to all; for as long as the worst and
the best have not been defined in terms of a clearly and concretely
conceived ideal, and then the precise margin of possibilities determined, we do not know which is the lesser evil, and consequently we
are compelled to accept under this name anything effectively imposed
by those who dispose of force, since any existing evil whatever is
always less than the possible evils which uncalculating action invariably
runs the risk of bringing about. Broadly speaking, blind men such as
we are in these days have only the choice between surrender and
adventure. And yet we cannot avoid the duty of determining here and
now the attitude to adopt with regard to the present situation. That is
why, until we have—if, indeed, such a thing is possible—taken to

pieces the social mechanism, it is permissible perhaps to try to outline its principles; provided it be clearly understood that such a rough sketch rules out any kind of categorical assertion, and aims solely at submitting a few ideas, by way of hypotheses, to the critical examination of honest people. Besides, we are far from being without a guide on the subject. If Marx's system, in its broad outlines, is of little assistance, it is a different matter when it comes to the analyses he was led to make by the concrete study of capitalism, and in which, while believing that he was limiting himself to describing a system, he probably more than once seized upon the hidden nature of oppression itself.

Among all the forms of social organization which history has to show, there are very few which appear to be really free from oppression; and these few are not very well known. All of them correspond to an extremely low level of production, so low that the division of labour is pretty well unknown, except between the sexes, and each family produces little more than its own requirements. It is sufficiently obvious, moreover, that such material conditions necessarily rule out oppression, since each man, compelled to sustain himself personally, is continually at grips with outside nature; war itself at this stage, is war of pillage and extermination, not of conquest, because the means of consolidating a conquest and especially of turning it to account are lacking. What is surprising is not that oppression should make its appearance only after higher forms of economy have been reached, but that it should always accompany them. This means, therefore, that as between a completely primitive economy and more highly developed forms of economy there is a difference not only of degree, but also of kind. And, in fact, although from the point of view of consumption there is but a change-over to slightly better conditions, production, which is the decisive factor, is itself transformed in its very essence. This transformation consists at first sight in a progressive emancipation with respect to nature. In completely primitive forms of production— hunting, fishing, gathering—human effort appears as a simple reaction to the inexorable pressure continually exercised on man by nature, and that in two ways. To start with, it takes place, to all intents and purposes, under immediate compulsion, under the ever-present spur of natural needs; and, by an indirect consequence, the action seems to receive its form from nature herself owing to the important part played therein by an intuition comparable to animal instinct and a patient observation of the most frequent natural phenomena, also owing to the indefinite repetition of methods that have often succeeded without men's knowing why, and which are doubtless regarded as being welcomed by nature with special favour. At this stage, each man is necessarily free with respect to other men, because he is in direct contact with the conditions of his own existence, and because nothing human interposes itself between them and him; but, on the other hand, and to the same extent, he is narrowly subjected to nature's dominion, and he shows this clearly enough by deifying her. At higher stages of production, nature's compulsion continues certainly to be exercised, and still pitilessly, but in an apparently less immediate fashion; it seems to become more and more liberalized and to leave an increasing margin to man's freedom of choice, to his faculty of initiative and decision. Action is no longer tied moment by moment to nature's exigencies; men learn how to store up reserves on a long-term basis for meeting needs not yet actually felt; efforts which can be only of indirect usefulness become more and more numerous; at the same time a systematic co-ordination in time and in space becomes possible and necessary, and its importance increases continually. In short, man seems to pass by stages, with respect to nature, from servitude to dominion. At the same time nature gradually loses her divine character, and divinity more and more takes on human shape. Unfortunately, this emancipation is only a flattering semblance. In reality, at these higher stages, human action continues, as a whole, to be nothing but pure obedience to the brutal spur of an immediate necessity; only, instead of being harried by nature, man is henceforth harried by man. However, it is still the same pressure exerted by nature that continues to make itself felt, although indirectly; for oppression is exercised by force, and in the long run all force originates in nature.

The notion of force is far from simple, and yet it is the first that has to be elucidated in order to formulate the problems of society. Force and oppression—that makes two; but what needs to be understood above all is that it is not the manner in which use is made of some particular force, but its very nature, which determines whether it is oppressive or not. Marx clearly perceived this in connection with the State; he understood that this machine for grinding men down, cannot stop grinding as long as it goes on functioning, no matter in whose hands it may be. But this insight has a far more general application. Oppression proceeds exclusively from objective conditions. The first of these is the existence of privileges; and it is not men's laws or decrees which determine privileges, nor yet titles to property; it is the very nature of things. Certain circumstances, which correspond to stages, no doubt inevitable, in human development, give rise to forces which come between the ordinary man and his own conditions of existence, between the effort and the fruit of the effort, and which are, inherently, the monopoly of a few, owing to the fact that they cannot be shared among all; thenceforward these privileged beings, although they depend, in order to live, on the work of others, hold in their hands the fate of the very people on whom they depend, and equality is destroyed. This is what happens to begin with when the religious rites by which man thinks to win nature over to his side, having become too numerous and complicated to be known by all, finally become the secret and consequently the monopoly of a few priests; the priest then disposes, albeit only through a fiction, of all of nature's powers, and it is in their name that he exercises authority. Nothing essential is changed when this monopoly is no longer made up of rites but of scientific processes, and when those in possession of it are called scientists and technicians instead of priests.

Arms, too, give rise to a privilege from the day when, on the one hand, they are sufficiently powerful to render any defence by unarmed against armed men impossible, and, on the other, the handling of them has become sufficiently advanced, and consequently difficult, to require a long apprenticeship and continuous practice. For henceforth the workers are powerless to defend themselves, whereas the warriors, albeit incapable of production, always take forcible possession of the fruits of other people's labour; the workers are thus at the mercy of the warriors, and not the other way about. The same thing applies to gold, and more generally to money, as soon as the division of labour is so far developed that no worker can live off his own products without having exchanged at any rate some of them for those of others; the organization of exchange then becomes necessarily the monopoly of a few specialists who, having money under their control, can both obtain for themselves, in order to live, the products of others' labour, and at the same time deprive the producers of the indispensably necessary.

In short, wherever, in the struggle against men or against nature, efforts need to be multiplied and co-ordinated to be effective, co-ordination becomes the monopoly of a few leaders as soon as it reaches a certain degree of complexity, and execution's primary law is then obedience; this is true both for the management of public affairs and for that of private undertakings. There may be other sources of privilege, but these are the chief ones; furthermore, except in the case of money, which appears at a given moment of history, all these factors enter into play under all systems of oppression; what changes is the way in which they are distributed and combined, the degree of concentration of power, and also the more or less closed and consequently more or less mysterious character of each monopoly. Nevertheless, privileges, of themselves, are not sufficient to cause oppression. Inequality could be easily mitigated by the resistance of the weak and the feeling for justice of the strong; it would not lead to a still harsher form of necessity than that of natural needs themselves, were it not for the intervention of a further factor, namely, the struggle for power.

As Marx clearly understood in the case of capitalism, and as a few moralists have perceived in a more general way, power contains a sort of fatality which weighs as pitilessly on those who command as on those who obey; nay more, it is in so far as it enslaves the former that, through their agency, it presses down upon the latter. The struggle against nature entails certain inescapable necessities which nothing can turn aside, but these necessities contain within themselves their own limits; nature resists, but she does not defend herself and where she alone is involved, each situation presents certain well-defined obstacles which arouse the best in human effort. It is altogether different as soon as relations between man and man take the place of direct contact between man and nature. The preservation of power is a vital necessity for the powerful, since it is their power which provides their sustenance; but they have to preserve it both against their rivals and against their inferiors, and these latter cannot do otherwise than try to rid themselves of dangerous masters; for, through a vicious circle, the master produces fear in the slave by the very fact that he is afraid of him, and vice versa; and the same is true as between rival powers.

What is more, the two struggles that every man of power has to wage—first against those over whom he rules, secondly against his rivals—are inextricably bound up together and each is all the time rekindling the other. A power, whatever it may be, must always tend towards strengthening itself at home by means of successes gained abroad, for such successes provide it with more powerful means of coercion; besides, the struggle against its rivals rallies behind it its own slaves, who are under the illusion they have a personal interest in the result of the battle. But, in order to obtain from the slaves the obedience and sacrifices indispensable to victory, that power has to make itself more oppressive; to be in a position to exercise this oppression, it is still more imperatively compelled to turn outwards; and so on. We can follow out the same chain of events by starting from another link; show how a given social group, in order to be in a position to defend itself against the outside powers threatening to lay hands on it, must itself submit to an oppressive form of authority; how the power thus set up, in order to maintain its position, must stir up conflicts with rival powers; and so on, once again. Thus it is that the most fatal of vicious circles drags the whole society in the wake of its masters in a mad merry-go-round.

There are only two ways of breaking the circle, either by abolishing inequality, or else by setting up a stable power, a power such that there exists a balance between those who command and those who obey. It is this second solution that has been sought by all whom we call upholders of order, or at any rate all those among them who have been moved neither by servility nor by ambition; it was doubtless so with the Latin writers who praised "the immense majesty of the Roman peace", with Dante, with the reactionary school at the beginning of the nineteenth century, with Balzac, and is so today with sincere and thoughtful men of the Right. But this stability of power—objective of those who call themselves realists—shows itself to be a chimera, if one examines it closely, on the same grounds as the anarchists' utopia.

Between man and matter, each action, whether successful or not, establishes a balance that can only be upset from outside; for matter is inert. A displaced stone accepts its new position; the wind consents to guide to her destination the same ship which it would have sent off her course if sails and rudder had not been properly adjusted. But men are essentially active beings and have a faculty of self-determination which they can never renounce, even should they so desire, except on the day when, through death, they drop back into the state of inert matter; so that every victory won over men contains within itself the germ of a possible defeat, unless it goes as far as extermination. But extermination abolishes power by abolishing its object. Thus there is, in the very essence of power, a fundamental contradiction that prevents it from ever existing in the true sense of the word; those who are called the masters, ceaselessly compelled to reinforce their power for fear of seeing it snatched away from them, are for ever seeking a dominion essentially impossible to attain; beautiful illustrations of this search are offered by the infernal torments in Greek mythology. It would be otherwise if one man could possess in himself a force superior to that of many other men put together; but such is never the case; the instruments of power—arms, gold, machines, magical or technical secrets— always exist independently of him who disposes of them, and can be taken up by others. Consequently all power is unstable.

Generally speaking, among human beings, since the relationships between rulers and ruled are never fully acceptable, they always constitute an irremediable disequilibrium which is continually aggravating itself; the same is true even in the sphere of private life, where love, for example, destroys all balance in the soul as soon as it seeks to dominate or to be dominated by its object. But here at any rate there is nothing external to prevent reason from returning and putting everything to rights by establishing liberty and equality; whereas social relationships, in so far as the very methods of labour and of warfare rule out equality, seem to cause madness to weigh down on mankind in the manner of an external fatality. For, owing to the fact that there is never power, but only a race for power, and that there is no term, no limit, no proportion set to this race, neither is there any limit or proportion set to the efforts that it exacts; those who give themselves up to it, compelled to do always better than their rivals, who in their turn strive to do better than they, must sacrifice not only the existence of the slaves, but their own also and that of their nearest and dearest; so it is that Agamemnon sacrificing his daughter lives again in the capitalists who, to maintain their privileges, acquiesce lightheartedly in wars that may rob them of their sons.

Thus the race for power enslaves everybody, strong and weak alike. Marx saw this clearly with reference to the capitalist system. Rosa Luxemburg used to inveigh against the aspect of "aimless merry-go-round" presented by the Marxist picture of capitalist accumulation, that picture in which consumption appears as a "necessary evil" to be reduced to the minimum, a mere means for keeping alive those who devote themselves, whether as leaders or as workers, to the supreme object, which is none other than the manufacture of capital equipment, that is to say of the means of production. And yet it is the profound absurdity of this picture which gives it its profound truth; a truth which extends singularly beyond the framework of the capitalist system. The only characteristic peculiar to this system is that the instruments of industrial production are at the same time the chief weapons in the race for power; but always the methods pursued in the race for power, whatever they may be, bring men under their subjection through the same frenzy and impose themselves on them as absolute ends. It is the reflection of this frenzy that lends an epic grandeur to works such as the *Comédie Humaine*, Shakespeare's *Histories*, the *chansons de geste*, or the *Iliad*. The real subject of the *Iliad* is the sway exercised by war over the warriors, and, through them, over humanity in general; none of them knows why each sacrifices himself and all his family to a bloody and aimless war, and that is why, all through the poem, it is the gods who are credited with the mysterious influence which nullifies peace negotiations, continually revives hostilities, and brings together again the contending forces urged by a flash of good sense to abandon the struggle.

Thus in this ancient and wonderful poem there already appears the essential evil besetting humanity, the substitution of means for ends. At times war occupies the forefront, at other times the search for wealth, at other times production; but the evil remains the same. The common run of moralists complain that man is moved by his private interest: would to heaven it were so! Private interest is a self-centred principle of action, but at the same time restricted, reasonable and incapable of giving rise to unlimited evils. Whereas, on the other hand, the law of all activities governing social life, except in the case of primitive communities, is that here each one sacrifices human life—in himself and in others—to things which are only means to a better way of living. This sacrifice takes on various forms, but it all comes back to the question of power. Power, by definition, is only a means; or to put it better, to possess a power is simply to possess means of action which exceed the very limited force that a single individual has at his disposal. But power-seeking, owing to its essential incapacity to seize hold of its object, rules out all consideration of an end, and finally comes, through an inevitable reversal, to take the place of all ends. It is this reversal of the relationship between means and end, it is this funda-mental folly that accounts for all that is senseless and bloody right through history. Human history is simply the history of the servitude which makes men—oppressors and oppressed alike—the plaything of the instruments of domination they themselves have manufactured, and thus reduces living humanity to being the chattel of inanimate chattels.

Thus it is things, not men, that prescribe the limits and laws govern-ing this giddy race for power. Men's desires are powerless to control it. The masters may well dream of moderation, but they are prohibited from practising this virtue, on pain of defeat, except to a very slight extent; so that, apart from a few almost miraculous exceptions, such as Marcus Aurelius, they quickly become incapable even of conceiving it. As for the oppressed, their permanent revolt, which is always simmer-ing, though it only breaks out now and then, can operate in such a way as to aggravate the evil as well as to restrict it; and on the whole it rather constitutes an aggravating factor in that it forces the masters to make their power weigh ever more heavily for fear of losing it.

From time to time the oppressed manage to drive out one team of oppressors and to replace it by another, and sometimes even to change the form of oppression; but as for abolishing oppression itself that would first mean abolishing the sources of it, abolishing all the mon-opolies, the magical and technical secrets that give a hold over nature, armaments, money, co-ordination of labour. Even if the oppressed were sufficiently conscious to make up their minds to do so, they could not succeed. It would be condemning themselves to immediate enslavement by the social groupings that had not carried out the same change; and even were this danger to be miraculously averted, it would be condemning themselves to death, for, once men have forgotten the methods of primitive production and have transformed the natural environment into which these fitted, they cannot recover immediate contact with nature.

It follows that, in spite of so many vague desires to put an end to madness and oppression, the concentration of power and the aggravation of its tyrannical character would know no bounds were these not by good fortune found in the nature of things. It behoves us to determine roughly what these bounds can be; and for this purpose we must keep in mind the fact that, if oppression is a necessity of social life, this necessity has nothing providential about it. It is not because it becomes detrimental to production that oppression can come to an end; the "revolt of the productive forces", so naïvely invoked by Trotsky as a factor in history, is a pure fiction. We should be mistaken likewise in assuming that oppression to be ineluctable as soon as the productive forces have been sufficiently developed to ensure welfare and leisure for all. Aristotle admitted that there would no longer be anything to stand in the way of the abolition of slavery if it were possible to have the indispensable jobs done by "mechanical slaves", and when Marx attempted to forecast the future of the human species, all he did was to take up this idea and develop it. It would be true if men were guided by considerations of welfare; but from the days of the *Iliad* to our own times, the senseless demands made by the struggle for power have taken away even the leisure for thinking about welfare. The raising of the output of human effort will remain powerless to lighten the load of this effort as long as the social structure implies the reversal of the relationship between means and ends, in other words, as long as the methods of labour and of warfare give to a few men a discretionary power over the masses; for the fatigues and privations that have become unnecessary in the struggle against nature will be absorbed by the war carried on between men for the defence or acquisition of privileges. Once society is divided up into men who command and men who execute, the whole of social life is governed by the struggle for power, and the struggle for subsistence only enters in as one factor, indispensable to be sure, of the former.

The Marxist view, according to which social existence is determined by the relations between man and nature established by production, certainly remains the only sound basis for any historical investigation; only these relations must be considered first of all in terms of the problem of power, the means of subsistence forming simply one of the data of this problem. This order seems absurd, but it merely reflects the essential absurdity lying at the very heart of social life. A scientific study of history would thus be a study of the actions and reactions which are perpetually arising between the organization of power and the methods of production; for although power depends on the material conditions of life, it never ceases to transform these conditions themselves. Such a study goes very far beyond our possibilities at the moment; but before grappling with the infinite complexity of the facts, it is useful to make an abstract diagram of this interplay of actions and reactions, rather in the same way as astronomers have had to invent an imaginary celestial sphere so as to find their way about among the movements and positions of the stars.

We must try first of all to draw up a list of the inevitable necessities which limit all species of power. In the first place, any sort of power relies upon instruments which have in each situation a given scope. Thus you do not command in the same way, by means of soldiers armed with bows and arrows, spears and swords as you do by means of aeroplanes and incendiary bombs; the power of gold depends on the role played by exchanges in economic life; that of technical secrets is measured by the difference between what you can accomplish with their aid and what you can accomplish without them; and so on. As a matter of fact, one must always include in this balance-sheet the subterfuges by which the powerful obtain through persuasion what they are totally unable to obtain by force, either by placing the oppressed in a situation such that they have or think they have an immediate interest in doing what is asked of them, or by inspiring them with a fanaticism calculated to make them accept any and every sacrifice. Secondly, since the power that a human being really exercises extends only to what is effectively under his control, power is always running up against the actual limits of the controlling faculty, and these are extremely narrow. For no single mind can encompass a whole mass of ideas at once; no man can be in several places at once; and for master and slave alike there are never more than twenty-four hours in a day. Collaboration apparently constitutes a remedy for this drawback; but as it is never absolutely free from rivalry, it gives rise to infinite complications. The faculties of examining, comparing, weighing, deciding, combining are essentially individual, and consequently the same thing applies also to power, whose exercise is inseparable from these faculties; collective power is a fiction, at any rate in final analysis. As for the number of interests that can come under the control of one single man, that depends to a very large extent on individual factors such as breadth and quickness of intelligence, capacity for work, firmness of character; but it also depends on the objective conditions of the control exercised, more or less rapid methods of transport and communication, simplicity or otherwise of the machinery of power. Lastly, the exercise of any form of power is subject to the existence of a surplus in the production of commodities, and a sufficiently large surplus so that all those engaged, whether as masters or as slaves, in the struggle for power, may be able to live. Obviously, the extent of such surplus depends on the methods of production, and consequently also on the social organization. Here, therefore, are three factors that enable one to conceive political and social power as constituting at each moment something analogous to a measurable force. However, in order to complete the picture, one must bear in mind that the men who find themselves in relationship, whether as masters or as slaves, with the phenomenon of power are unconscious of this analogy. The powerful, be they priests, military leaders, kings or capitalists, always believe that they command by divine right; and those who are under them feel themselves crushed by a power which seems to them either divine or diabolical, but in any case supernatural. Every oppressive society is cemented by this religion of power, which falsifies all social relations by enabling the powerful to command over and above what they are able to impose; it is only otherwise in times of popular agitation, times when, on the contrary, all—rebellious slaves and threatened masters alike—forget how heavy and how solid the chains of oppression are.

Thus a scientific study of history ought to begin by analysing the reactions brought to bear at each moment by power on the conditions which assign to it objectively its limits; and a hypothetical sketch of the play of these reactions is indispensable in order to conduct such an analysis, far too difficult, incidentally, considering our present possibilities. Some of these reactions are conscious and willed. Every power consciously strives, in proportion to the means at its disposal—a proportion determined by the social organization—to improve production and official control within its own sphere; history offers many an example of this, from the Pharaohs down to the present day, and it is on this that the notion of enlightened despotism is founded. On the other hand, every power strives also, and again consciously, to destroy among its competitors the means whereby to produce and govern, and is the object on their part of a similar attempt. Thus the struggle for power is at the same time constructive and destructive, and brings about economic progress or decadence, depending on whichever aspect wins the day; and it is clear that in a given civilization destruction will take place to an extent all the greater the more difficult it is for a power to expand without coming up against rival powers approximately as strong as itself. But the indirect consequences of the exercise of power are far more important than the conscious efforts of the wielders of power.

Every power, from the mere fact that it is exercised, extends to the farthest possible limit the social relations on which it is based; thus military power multiplies wars, commercial capital multiplies exchanges. Now it sometimes happens, through a sort of providential accident, that this extension gives rise, by some mechanism or other, to new resources that make a new extension possible, and so on, more or less in the same way as food strengthens living beings in full process of growth and enables them thus to win still more food so as to acquire still greater strength. All régimes provide examples of such providential accidents; for without them no form of power could endure, and consequently those powers that benefit from them are the only ones to subsist. Thus war enabled the Romans to carry off slaves, that is to say workers in the prime of life, whom others had had to provide for during childhood; the profit derived from slave labour made it possible to reinforce the army, and the stronger army undertook more important wars which brought in new and bigger consignments of slaves as booty. Similarly, the roads which the Romans built for military purposes later facilitated the government and exploitation of the conquered provinces, and thus contributed towards storing up resources for future wars.

If we turn now to modern times, we see, for example, that the extension of exchanges has brought about a greater division of labour, which in its turn has made a wider circulation of commodities indispensable; furthermore, the increased productivity which has resulted from this has furnished new resources that have been able to transform themselves into commercial and industrial capital. As far as big industry is concerned, it is clear that each important advance in mechanization has created at the same time resources, instruments and a stimulus towards a further advance. Similarly, it was the technique of big industry which came to provide the means of control and information indispensable to the centralized economy that is the inevitable outcome of big industry, such as the telegraph, the telephone, the daily press. The same may be said with regard to the means of transport. One could find all through history an immense number of similar examples, bearing on the widest and the narrowest aspects of social life. One may define the growth of a system by the fact that all it needs to do is to function in order to create new resources enabling it to function on a larger scale.

This phenomenon of automatic development is so striking that one would be tempted to imagine that a happily constituted system, if one may so express it, would go on enduring and progressing endlessly. That is exactly what the nineteenth century, socialists included, imagined with regard to the system of big industry. But if it is easy to imagine in a vague way an oppressive system that would never fall into decadence, it is no longer the same if one wants to conceive clearly and concretely the indefinite extension of a specific power. If it could extend endlessly its means of control, it would tend indefinitely towards a limit which would be something like ubiquity; if it could extend its resources endlessly, everything would be as though surrounding nature were evolving gradually towards that unqualified abundance from which Adam and Eve benefited in the earthly paradise; and, finally, if it could extend indefinitely the range of its own instruments—whether it be a question of arms, gold, technical secrets, machines or anything else—it would tend towards abolishing that correlation which, by indissolubly linking together the notions of master and of slave, establishes between master and slave a relationship of mutual dependence.

One cannot prove that all this is impossible; but one must assume that it is impossible, or else decide to think of human history as a fairytale. In general, one can only regard the world in which we live as subject to laws if one admits that every phenomenon in it is limited; and it is the same for the phenomenon of power, as Plato had understood. If we want to consider power as a conceivable phenomenon, we must think that it can extend the foundations on which it rests up to a certain point only, after which it comes up, as it were, against an impassable wall. But even so it is not in a position to stop; the spur of competition forces it to go ever farther and farther, that is to say to go beyond the limits within which it can be effectively exercised. It extends beyond what it is able to control; it commands over and above what it can impose; it spends in excess of its own resources. Such is the internal contradiction which every oppressive system carries within itself like a seed of death; it is made up of the opposition between the necessarily limited character of the material bases of power and the necessarily unlimited character of the race for power considered as relationship between men.

For as soon as a power goes beyond the limits assigned to it by the nature of things, it narrows down the bases on which it rests, renders these limits themselves narrower and narrower. By spreading beyond what it is able to control, it breeds a parasitism, a waste, a confusion which, once they have appeared, increase automatically. By attempting to command where actually it is not in a position to compel obedience, it provokes reactions which it can neither foresee nor deal with. Finally, by wishing to spread the exploitation of the oppressed beyond what the objective resources make possible, it exhausts these resources themselves; this is doubtless what is meant by the ancient and popular tale of the goose with the golden eggs. Whatever may be the sources from whence the exploiters draw the material goods which they appropriate, a day arrives when such and such a method of development, which was at first, as it went on spreading, more and more productive, finally becomes, on the other hand, increasingly costly. That is how the Roman army, which had first of all brought wealth to Rome, ended by ruining it; that is how the knights of the Middle Ages, whose battles had first of all brought a relative security to the peasants, who found themselves to a certain extent protected against acts of brigandage, ended in the course of their interminable wars by laying waste the countryside which fed them; and it certainly seems as though capitalism is passing through a phase of this kind. Once more, it cannot be proved that it must always be so; but it has to be assumed, unless the possibility of inexhaustible resources is also assumed. Thus it is the nature itself of things which constitutes that justice-dealing divinity the Greeks worshipped under the name of Nemesis, and which punishes excess.

When a specific form of domination finds itself thus arrested in its development and faced with decadence, it does not follow that it begins to disappear progressively; sometimes it is then, on the contrary, that it becomes most harshly oppressive, that it crushes human beings under its weight, that it grinds down body, heart and spirit without mercy. However, since everyone begins little by little to feel the lack of the resources required by some to maintain their supremacy, by others to live, a time comes when, on every hand, there is a feverish search for expedients. There is no reason why such a search should not remain fruitless; and in that case the régime can only end by collapsing for want of the means of subsistence and being replaced, not by another and better organised régime, but by a disorder, a poverty, a primitive condition of existence which continue until some new factor or other gives rise to new relationships of force. If it happens otherwise, if the search for new material resources is successful, new patterns of social life arise and a change of régime begins to form slowly and, as it were, subterraneously. Subterraneously, because these new forms can only develop in so far as they are compatible with the established order and do not represent, in appearance at any rate, any danger for the powers that be; otherwise nothing could prevent these powers from destroying them, as long as they remain the stronger. For the new social patterns to triumph over the old, this continued development must already have brought them to play effectively a more important role in the functioning of the social organism; in other words, they must have given rise to more powerful forces than those at the disposal of the official authorities. Thus there is never really any break in continuity, not even when the change of régime seems to be the result of a bloody struggle; for all that victory then does is to sanction forces that, even before the struggle, were the decisive factor in the life of the community, social patterns that had long since begun gradually to replace those on which the declining régime rested. So it was that, under the Roman Empire, the barbarians had begun to occupy the most important posts, the army was disintegrating little by little into armed bands led by adventurers, and the system of military colonies gradually replaced slavery by serfdom—all this long before the great invasions. Similarly, the French bourgeoisie did not by any means wait until 1789 to get the better of the nobility. The Russian Revolution, thanks to a singular conjunction of circumstances, certainly seemed to give rise to something entirely new; but the truth is that the privileges it abolished had not for a long time rested on any social foundation other than tradition; that the institutions arising out of the insurrection did not perhaps effectively function for as long as a single morning; and that the real forces, namely big industry, the police, the army, the bureaucracy, far from being smashed by the Revolution, attained, thanks to it, a power unknown in other countries.

Generally speaking, the sudden reversal of the relationship between forces which is what we usually understand by the term "revolution" is not only a phenomenon unknown in history, but furthermore, if we examine it closely, something literally inconceivable, for it would be a victory of weakness over force, the equivalent of a balance whose lighter scale were to go down. What history offers us is slow trans-formations of régimes, in which the bloody events to which we give the name "revolutions" play a very secondary role, and from which they may even be absent; such is the case when the social class which ruled in the name of the old relationships of force manages to keep a part of the power under cover of the new relationships, and the history of England supplies an example. But whatever may be the patterns taken by social transformations, all one finds, if one tries to lay bare the mechanism, is a dreary play of blind forces that unite together or clash, that progress or decline, that replace each other, without ever ceasing to grind beneath them the unfortunate race of human beings. At first sight there seems to be no weak spot in this sinister mesh of circumstances through which an attempt at deliverance might find its way. But it is not from such a vague, abstract and miserably hasty sketch as this that one can claim to draw any conclusion.

We must pose once again the fundamental problem, namely, what constitutes the bond which seems hitherto to have united social oppression and progress in the relations between man and nature? If one considers human development as a whole up to our own time, if, above all, one contrasts primitive tribes, organized practically without inequality, with our present-day civilization, it seems as if man cannot manage to lighten the yoke imposed by natural necessities without an equal increase in the weight of that imposed by social oppression, as though by the play of a mysterious equilibrium. And even, what is stranger still, it would seem that if, in fact, the human collectivity has to a large extent freed itself from the crushing burden which the gigantic forces of nature place on frail humanity, it has, on the other hand, taken in some sort nature's place to the point of crushing the individual in a similar manner.

What makes primitive man a slave? The fact that he hardly orders his own activity at all; he is the plaything of need, which dictates each of his movements or very nearly, and harries him with its relentless spur; and his actions are regulated not by his own intelligence, but by the customs and caprices—both equally incomprehensible—of a nature that he can but worship with blind submission. If we consider simply the collectivity, men seem nowadays to have raised themselves to a condition that is diametrically the opposite of that servile state. Hardly a single one of their tasks constitutes a mere response to the imperative impulsion of need; work is accomplished in such a way as to take charge of nature and to organize her so that needs can be satisfied. Humanity no longer believes itself to be in the presence of capricious divinities whose good graces must be won over; it knows that it has merely to handle inert matter, and acquits itself of this task by methodically following out clearly conceived laws. At last we seem to have reached that epoch predicted by Descartes when men would use "the force and actions of fire, water, air, the stars and all the other bodies" in the same way as they do the artisans' tools, and would thus make themselves masters of nature. But, by a strange inversion, this collective dominion transforms itself into servitude as soon as one descends to the scale of the individual, and into a servitude fairly closely resembling that associated with primitive conditions of existence.

The efforts of the modern worker are imposed on him by a constraint as brutal, as pitiless and which holds him in as tight a grip as hunger does the primitive hunter. From the time of that primitive hunter up to that of the worker in our large factories, passing by way of the Egyptian workers driven by the lash, the slaves of antiquity, the serfs of the Middle Ages constantly threatened by the seigniorial sword, men have never ceased to be goaded to work by some outside force and on pain of almost immediate death. And as for the sequence of movements in work, that, too, is often imposed from outside on our workers, exactly as in the case of primitive men, and is as mysterious for the ones as it was for the others; what is more, in this respect, the constraint is in certain cases incomparably more brutal today than it has ever been. However tied and bound a primitive man was to routine and blind gropings, he could at least try to think things out, to combine and innovate at his own risk, a liberty which is absolutely denied to a worker engaged in a production line. Lastly, if humanity appears to have reached the stage of controlling those forces of nature which, however, in Spinoza's words, "infinitely surpass those of mankind"— and that in almost as sovereign a fashion as a rider controls his horse— that victory does not belong to men taken individually; only the largest collectivities are in a position to handle "the force and actions of fire, water, . . . and all the other bodies that surround us"; as for the members of these collectivities, both oppressors and oppressed are alike subjected to the implacable demands of the struggle for power.

Thus, in spite of progress, man has not emerged from the servile condition in which he found himself when he was handed over weak and naked to all the blind forces that make up the universe; it is merely that the power which keeps him on his knees has been as it were transferred from inert matter to the human society of which he is a member. That is why it is this society which is imposed on his worship through all the various forms that religious feeling takes in turn. Hence the social question poses itself in a fairly clear manner; the mechanism of this transfer must be examined; we must try to find out why man has had to pay this price for his power over nature; form an idea of what would constitute the least unhappy position for him to be in, that is to say the one in which he would be the least enslaved to the twin domination of nature and society; and lastly, discern what roads can lead towards such a position, and what instruments present-day civilization could place in men's hands if they aspired to transform their lives in this way.

We accept material progress too easily as a gift of the gods, as something which goes without saying; we must look fairly and squarely at the conditions at the cost of which it takes place. Primitive life is something easy to understand; man is spurred on by hunger, or at any rate by the anguished thought that he will soon go hungry, and he sets off in search of food; he shivers in the cold, or at any rate at the thought that he will soon feel cold, and he goes in search of heat-creating or heat-preserving materials; and so on. As for the way in which to set about the matter, this is given him in the first place by the habit acquired in childhood of imitating his seniors, and also as a result of the habits which he has given himself in the course of innumerable tentative efforts, by repeating those methods which have succeeded; when caught off his guard, he continues to proceed by trial and error, spurred on as he is to act by a sharp urge which never leaves him a moment's peace. In all this process, man has only to yield to his own nature, not master it.

On the other hand, as soon as we pass to a more advanced stage of civilization, everything becomes miraculous. Men are then found laying by things that are good to consume, desirable things, which they nevertheless go without. They are found giving up to a large extent the search for food, warmth, etc., and spending the best part of their energy on apparently unprofitable labours. As a matter of fact, most of these labours, far from being unprofitable, are infinitely more profitable than the efforts of primitive man, for they result in an organization of outside nature in a manner favourable to human existence; but this efficacy is indirect and often separated from the actual effort by so many intermediaries that the mind has difficulty in covering them; it is a long-term efficacy, often so long-term that it is only future generations which will benefit from it; while, on the other hand, the utter fatigue, physical pains and dangers connected with these labours are felt immediately, and all the time. Now, everybody knows from his own experience how unusual it is for an abstract idea having a long-term utility to triumph over present pains, needs and desires. It must, however, do so in the matter of social existence, on pain of a regression to a primitive form of life.

But what is more miraculous still is the co-ordination of labour. Any reasonably high level of production presupposes a more or less extensive co-operation; and co-operation shows itself in the fact that the efforts of each one have meaning and efficacy only through their relationship to and exact correspondence with the efforts of all the rest, in such a way that all the efforts together form one single collective piece of work. In other words, the movements of several men must be combined according to the manner in which the movements of a single man are combined. But how can this be done? A combination can only take place if it is intellectually conceived; while a relationship is never formed except within one mind. The number 2 thought of by one man cannot be added to the number 2 thought of by another man so as to make up the number 4; similarly, the idea that one of the co-operators has of the partial work he is carrying out cannot be combined with the idea that each of the others has of his respective task so as to form a coherent piece of work. Several human minds cannot become united in one collective mind, and the expressions "collective soul", "collective thought", so commonly employed nowadays, are altogether devoid of meaning. Consequently, for the efforts of several to be combined, they all need to be directed by one and the same mind, as the famous line in Faust expresses it: "One mind is enough for a thousand hands."

In the egalitarian organization of primitive tribes, it is not possible to solve a single one of these problems, neither that of privation, nor that of incentive to effort, nor that of co-ordination of labour; on the other hand, social oppression provides an immediate solution, by creating, to put it broadly, two categories of men—those who command and those who obey. The leader co-ordinates without difficulty the efforts of those who are under his orders; he has no temptation to overcome in order to reduce them to what is strictly necessary; and as for the stimulus to effort, an oppressive organization is admirably equipped for driving men beyond the limit of their strength, some being whipped by ambition, others, in Homer's words, "under the goad of a harsh necessity".

The results are often extraordinary when the division between social categories is deep enough for those who decide what work shall be done never to be exposed to feeling or even knowing about the exhausting fatigue, the pains and the dangers of it, while those who do it and suffer have no choice, being continually under the sway of a more or less disguised menace of death. Thus it is that man escapes to a

certain extent from the caprices of blind nature only by handing
self over to the no less blind caprices of the struggle for power. T
never truer than when man reaches—as in our case—a technical
development sufficiently advanced to give him the mastery over the
forces of nature; for, in order that this may be so, co-operation has to
take place on such a vast scale that the leaders find they have to deal
with a mass of affairs which lie utterly beyond their capacity to control.
As a result, humanity finds itself as much the plaything of the forces of
nature, in the new form that technical progress has given them, as it
ever was in primitive times; we have had, are having, and will continue
to have bitter experience of this. As for attempts to preserve technique
while shaking off oppression, they at once provoke such laziness and
such confusion that those who have engaged in them are more often
than not obliged to place themselves again almost immediately under
the yoke; the experiment was tried out on a small scale in the producers' co-operatives, on a vast scale at the time of the Russian Revolution. It would seem that man is born a slave, and that servitude is his
natural condition.

THEORETICAL PICTURE OF A FREE SOCIETY

And yet nothing on earth can stop man from feeling himself born for
liberty. Never, whatever may happen, can he accept servitude; for he is
a thinking creature. He has never ceased to dream of a boundless liberty, whether as a past state of happiness of which a punishment has
deprived him, or as a future state of happiness that is due to him by
reason of a sort of pact with some mysterious providence. The communism imagined by Marx is the most recent form this dream has
taken. This dream has always remained vain, as is the case with all
dreams, or, if it has been able to bring consolation, this has only been
in the form of an opium; the time has come to give up dreaming of
liberty, and to make up one's mind to conceive it.

Perfect liberty is what we must try to represent clearly to ourselves,
not in the hope of attaining it, but in the hope of attaining a less
imperfect liberty than is our present condition; for the better can be
conceived only by reference to the perfect. One can only steer towards
an ideal. The ideal is just as unattainable as the dream, but differs from

the dream in that it concerns reality; it enables one, as a mathematical limit, to grade situations, whether real or realizable, in an order of value from least to greatest. Perfect liberty cannot be conceived as consisting merely in the disappearance of that necessity whose pressure weighs continually upon us; as long as man goes on existing, that is to say as long as he continues to constitute an infinitesimal fraction of this pitiless universe, the pressure exerted by necessity will never be relaxed for one single moment. A state of things in which man had as much enjoyment and as little fatigue as he liked can, except in fiction, find no place in the world in which we live. It is true that nature is milder or harsher towards human needs according to climate, and perhaps depending on the period; but to look expectantly for the miraculous invention that would render her mild everywhere, and once and for all, is about as reasonable as the hopes formerly placed in the year 1000. Besides, if we examine this fiction closely, it does not even seem that it is worth a single regret. We have only to bear in mind the weakness of human nature to understand that an existence from which the very notion of work had pretty well disappeared would be delivered over to the play of the passions and perhaps to madness; there is no self-mastery without discipline, and there is no other source of discipline for man than the effort demanded in overcoming external obstacles. A nation of idlers might well amuse itself by giving itself obstacles to overcome, exercise itself in the sciences, in the arts, in games; but the efforts that are the result of pure whim do not form for a man a means of controlling his own whims. It is the obstacles we encounter and that have to be overcome which give us the opportunity for self-conquest. Even the apparently freest forms of activity, science, art, sport, only possess value in so far as they imitate the accuracy, rigour, scrupulousness which characterize the performance of work, and even exaggerate them. Were it not for the model offered them unconsciously by the ploughman, the blacksmith, the sailor who work *comme il faut*—to use that admirably ambiguous expression—they would sink into the purely arbitrary. The only liberty that can be attributed to the Golden Age is that which little children would enjoy if parents did not impose rules on them; it is in reality only an unconditional surrender to caprice. The human body can in no case cease to depend on the mighty universe in which it is encased; even if man were to cease being subjected to material things and to his fellows by needs and dangers, he would only be more completely delivered into their hands by the emotions which would stir him continually to the depths of his soul, and against which no regular occupation would any longer protect him. If one were to understand by liberty the mere absence of all necessity, the word would be emptied of all concrete meaning but it would not then represent for us that which, when we are deprived of it, takes away the value from life.

One can understand by liberty something other than the possibility of obtaining without effort what is pleasureable. There exists a very different conception of liberty, an heroic conception which is that of common wisdom. True liberty is not defined by a relationship between desire and its satisfaction, but by a relationship between thought and action; the absolutely free man would be he whose every action proceeded from a preliminary judgment concerning the end which he set himself and the sequence of means suitable for attaining this end. It matters little whether the actions in themselves are easy or painful, or even whether they are crowned with success; pain and failure can make a man unhappy, but cannot humiliate him as long as it is he himself who disposes of his own capacity for action. And ordering one's own actions does not signify in any way acting arbitrarily; arbitrary actions do not proceed from any exercise of judgment, and cannot properly speaking be called free. Every judgment bears upon an objective set of circumstances, and consequently upon a warp and woof of necessities. Living man can on no account cease to be hemmed in on all sides by an absolutely inflexible necessity; but since he is a thinking creature, he can choose between either blindly submitting to the spur with which necessity pricks him on from outside, or else adapting himself to the inner representation of it that he forms in his own mind; and it is in this that the contrast between servitude and liberty lies.

The two terms of this contrast are, moreover, but ideal limits between which human life moves without ever being able to reach either, on pain of ceasing any longer to be life. A man would be completely a slave if all his movements proceeded from a source other than his mind, namely, either the irrational reactions of the body, or else the mind of other people; primitive man, ravenous, his every bound provoked by the spasms tearing at his belly, the Roman slave perpetually keyed up to execute the orders of an overseer armed with a whip, the manual worker of our own day engaged in a production line, all these approach that wretched condition. As for complete liberty, one can find an abstract model of it in a properly solved problem in arithmetic or geometry; for in a problem all the elements of the solution are given, and man can look for assistance only to his own judgment, alone capable of establishing between these elements the relationship which by itself constitutes the solution sought. The efforts and successes attending mathematics do not go beyond the compass of the sheet of paper, the realm of signs and figures; a completely free life would be one wherein all real difficulties presented themselves as kinds of problems, wherein all successes were as solutions carried into action. All the elements of success would then be given, that is to say known and able to be handled as are the mathematician's signs; to obtain the desired result it would be enough to place these elements in relation, thanks to the methodical direction the mind would impart, no longer to mere pen-strokes, but to effective movements that would leave their mark in the world. Or to put it better, the performance of any work whatever would consist in as conscious and as methodical a combination of efforts as can be the combination of numbers by which the solution of a problem is brought about when this solution results from reflection.

Man would then have his fate constantly in his own hands; at each moment he would forge the conditions of his own existence by an act of mind. Mere desire, it is true, would lead him nowhere; he would receive nothing gratuitously; and even the possibilities of effective effort would for him be strictly limited. But the very fact of not being able to obtain anything without having brought into action, in order to acquire it, all the powers of mind and body would enable man to tear himself away for good from the blind grip of the passions. A clear view of what is possible and what impossible, what is easy and what difficult, of the labours that separate the project from its accomplishment—this alone does away with insatiable desires and vain fears; from this and not from anything else proceed moderation and courage, virtues without which life is nothing but a disgraceful frenzy. Besides, the source of any kind of virtue lies in the shock produced by the human intelligence being brought up against a matter devoid of lenience and of falsity. It is not possible to conceive of a nobler destiny for man than that which brings him directly to grips with naked necessity, without his being able to expect anything except through his own exertions, and such that his life is a continual creation of himself by himself. Man is a limited being to whom it is not given to be, as in the case of the God of the theologians, the direct author of his own existence; but he would possess the human equivalent of that divine power if the material conditions that enable him to exist were exclusively the work of his mind directing the effort of his muscles. This would be true liberty.

Such liberty is only an ideal, and cannot be found in reality any more than a perfectly straight line can be drawn with a pencil. But it will be useful to conceive this ideal if we can discern at the same time what it is that separates us from it, and what are the circumstances that can cause us to move away from it or approach nearer to it. The first obstacle which appears is formed by the complexity and size of this world with which we have to deal: these infinitely outstrip our mental range. The difficulties of real life do not constitute problems made to our scale; they are like problems possessing an innumerable quantity of data, for matter is doubly indefinite, from the point of view of extent and from that of divisibility. That is why it is impossible for a human mind to take into account all the factors on which the success of what seems to be the simplest action depends; any given situation whatever leaves the door open to innumerable chance possibilities, and things escape our mind as water does between the fingers of our cupped hands. Hence it would seem that the mind is only able to exercise itself upon unreal combinations of signs, and that action must be reduced to the blindest form of groping. But, in fact, this is not so. It is true that we can never act with absolute certainty; but that does not matter so much as one might suppose. We can easily accept the fact that the results of our actions are dependent on accidents outside our control; what we must at all costs preserve from chance are our actions themselves, and that in such a way as to place them under the control of the mind. To achieve this, all that is necessary is that man should be able to conceive a chain of intermediaries linking the movements he is capable of to the results he wishes to obtain; and he can often do this, thanks to the relative stability that persists, athwart the blind cross-currents of the universe, on the scale of the human organism, and which alone enables that organism to subsist. It is true that this chain of intermediaries is never anything more than an abstract diagram; when one starts carrying out the action, accidents can arise at every moment to frustrate the most carefully drawn-up plans; but if the intelligence has been able clearly to elaborate the abstract plan of the action to be carried out, this means that it has managed, not of course to eliminate chance, but to give it a circumscribed and limited role, and, as it were, to filter it, by classifying with respect to this particular plan the undefined mass of possible accidents in a few clearly-defined series. Thus, the intelligence is powerless to get its bearings amid the innumerable eddies formed by wind and water on the high seas; but if we place in the midst of these swirling waters a boat whose sails and rudder are fixed in such and such a manner it is possible to draw up a list of the actions which they can cause it to undergo. All tools are thus, in a more or less perfect way, in the manner of instruments for defining chance events. Man could in this way eliminate chance, if not in his surroundings, at any rate within himself; however, even that is an unattainable ideal. The world is too full of situations whose complexity is beyond us for instinct, routine, trial and error, improvising ever to be able to cease playing a role in our labours; all man can do is to restrict this role more and more, thanks to scientific and technical progress. What matters is that this role should be subordinate and should not prevent method from constituting the very soul of work. It is also necessary that it should appear as provisional, and that routine and trial and error should always be regarded not as principles of action, but as make-shifts for the purpose of filling up the gaps in methodical conception; in this scientific hypotheses are a powerful aid by making us conceive half-understood phenomena as governed by laws comparable to those which determine the most clearly understood phenomena. And even in cases where we know nothing at all, we can still assume that similar laws are applicable; this is sufficient to eliminate, in default of ignorance, the feeling of mystery, and to make us understand that we live in a world in which man has only himself to look to for miracles.

There is, however, one source of mystery that we cannot eliminate, and which is none other than our own body. The extreme complexity of vital phenomena can perhaps be progressively unravelled, at any rate to a certain extent; but the immediate relationship linking our thoughts to our movements will always remain wrapped in impenetrable obscurity. In this sphere we cannot conceive any form of necessity, from the very fact that we cannot determine what are the intermediate links; moreover, the idea of necessity, as formed in the human mind, is, properly speaking, only applicable to matter. One cannot even discover in the phenomena in question, in default of a clearly conceivable necessity, an even approximate regularity. At times the reactions of the living body are completely foreign to the mind; at other times, but rarely, they simply carry out its orders; more often they accomplish what the mind has desired without the latter taking any part therein; often also they accompany the wishes formed in the mind without corresponding to them in any way; at other times again they precede the mind's thoughts. No classification is possible. That is why, when the movements of the living body play the major role in the struggle against nature, the very notion of necessity can with difficulty take shape; when these are successful, nature seems to be immediately obeying or complying with desires, and, when unsuccessful, to be rejecting them. This is what takes place in actions accomplished either without instruments or with instruments so well adapted to living members that all they do is to act as an extension of the natural movements of such. We can thus understand how primitive men, in spite of their very great dexterity in accomplishing all they have to do in order to continue to exist, visualize the relationship between man and the world under the aspect not of work but of magic. Between them and the web of necessities which constitutes nature and defines the real conditions of existence, all sorts of mysterious caprices, at whose mercy they believe themselves to be, henceforth interpose themselves in the manner of a screen; and however little oppressive the society which they form may be, they are none the less its slaves from the point of view of these imaginary caprices, often interpreted, furthermore, by priests and sorcerers of flesh and blood. These beliefs survive in the form of superstitions, and, contrary to what we like to think, no man is completely free from them; but their spell loses its potency in proportion as, in the struggle against nature, the living body assumes a secondary importance and passive instruments a primary importance. Such is the case when instruments, ceasing to be fashioned according to the structure of the human organism, force the latter, on the contrary, to adapt its movements to their own shape. Thenceforward there is no longer any correspondence between the motions to be carried out and the passions; the mind has to get away from desire and fear and apply itself solely to establishing an exact relationship between the movements imparted to the instruments and the objective aimed at. The docility of the body in such a case is a kind of miracle, but a miracle which the mind may ignore; the body, rendered as it were fluid through habit, to use Hegel's beautiful expression, simply causes the movements conceived in the mind to pass into the instruments. The attention is directed exclusively to the combinations formed by the movements of inert matter, and the idea of necessity appears in its purity, without any admixture of magic. For example, on dry land and borne along by the desires and fears that move his legs for him, man often finds that he has passed from one place to another without being aware of it; on the sea, on the other hand, as desires and fears have no hold over the boat, one has continually to use craft and strategy, set sails and rudder, transmute the thrust of the wind by means of a series of devices which can only be the work of a clear intelligence. You cannot entirely reduce the human body to this docile intermediary role between mind and instrument, but you can reduce it more and more to that role; this is what every technical advance helps to bring about.

But, unfortunately, even if you did manage strictly and in full detail to subject all forms of work without exception to methodical thought, a new obstacle to liberty would immediately arise on account of the profound difference in kind which separates theoretical speculation from action. In reality, there is nothing in common between the solution of a problem and the carrying out of an even perfectly methodical piece of work, between the sequence of ideas and the sequence of movements. The man who tackles a difficulty of a theoretical order proceeds by moving from what is simple to what is complex, from what is clear to what is obscure; the movements of the manual worker, on the other hand, are not some of them clearer and simpler than others, it is merely that those which come before are the condition of those which come after. Moreover, the mind more often than not musters together what execution has to separate, or separates what execution has to link up. That is why, when some piece of work or other presents the mind with difficulties that cannot immediately be overcome, it is impossible to combine the examination of these difficulties with the accomplishment of the work; the mind has first of all to solve the theoretical problem by its own particular methods, and afterwards the solution can be applied to the action. You cannot say in such a case that the action is, strictly speaking, methodical; it is in accordance with method, which is a very different thing. The difference is capital; for he who applies method has no need to conceive it in his mind at the moment he is applying it. Indeed, if it is a question of something complicated, he is unable to, even should he have elaborated it himself; for the attention, always forced to concentrate itself on the actual moment of execution, cannot embrace at the same time the series of relationships on which execution as a whole depends. Hence, what is carried out is not a conception but an abstract diagram indicating a sequence of movements, and as little penetrable by the mind, at the moment of execution, as is some formula resulting from mere routine or some magic rite. Moreover, one and the same conception is applicable, with or without modifications of detail, an indefinite number of times; for although the mind embraces at one stroke the series of possible applications of a given method, man is not thereby absolved from realizing them one by one every time that it is necessary. Thus for one single flash of thought there are an unlimited number of blind actions. It goes without saying that those who go on applying indefinitely such and such a method of work have often never given themselves the trouble of understanding it; furthermore, it frequently happens that each of them is only charged with a part of the job of execution, always the same, while his companions do the rest. Hence one is brought face to face with a paradoxical situation; namely, that there is method in the motions of work, but none in the mind of the worker. It would seem as though the method had transferred its abode from the mind into the matter. Automatic machines present the most striking image of this. From the moment when the mind which has worked out a method of action has no need to take part in the job of execution, this can be handed over to pieces of metal just as well as and better than to living members; and one is thus presented with the strange spectacle of machines in which the method has become so perfectly crystallized in metal that it seems as though it is they which do the thinkng, and it is the men who serve them who are reduced to the condition of automata.

Indeed, this contrast between the application and the understanding of the method is found again, in absolutely identical form, in the realm of pure theory itself. To take a simple example, it is absolutely impossible, at the moment when one is working out a difficult division sum, to have the theory of division present to the mind; and that is so not only because this theory, which is based on the relationship of division to multiplication, is of a certain complexity, but above all because when carrying out each of the partial operations at the end of which the division is accomplished, one forgets that the numbers represent now units, now tens, now hundreds. The signs combine together according to the laws governing the things which they signify; but, for want of being able to keep the relationship of sign to thing signified continually present to the mind, one handles them as though they combined together according to their own laws; and as a result the combinations become unintelligible, which means to say that they take place automatically. The mechanical nature of arithmetical operations is exemplified by the existence of calculating machines; but an accountant, too, is nothing else but an imperfect and unhappy calculating machine. Mathematics only progress by working in signs, by widening their significance, by creating signs of signs; thus the ordinary letters in algebra represent arbitrary quantities, or even virtual operations, as is the case with negative values; other letters stand for algebraic functions, and so on. As at each floor—if one may so express it—one inevitably loses sight of the relationship between sign and thing signified, the combinations of signs, although they remain rigorously methodical, very soon become impenetrable to the mind. No satisfactory algebraic machine exists, although several attempts have been made in this direction; but algebraic calculations are none the less more often than not as automatic as the work of an accountant. Or rather, they are more so in the sense that they are, in a way, essentially so. After working out a division, one can always ponder over it, while giving back the signs their significance, until one has understood the reason for each part of the operation; but it is not the same thing in algebra, where the signs, as a result of being handled and combined together as such, end by displaying an efficacy which their significance does not account for. Such are, for example, the signs e and i; by handling them suitably, one can smooth out all sorts of difficulties in a marvellous manner, and in particular if they are combined in a certain way with π, one arrives at the assertion that the squaring of the circle is impossible; and yet no mind in the world can conceive what connection the quantities—if one may call them such—that these letters designate can have with the problem of the squaring of the circle. The process of calculation places the signs in relation to one another on the sheet of paper, without the objects so signified being in relation in the mind; with the result that the actual question of the significance of signs ends by no longer possessing any meaning. One thus finds oneself in the position of having solved a problem by a species of magic, without the mind having connected the data with the solution. Consequently, here again, as in the case of the automatic machine, method seems to have material objects as its sphere instead of mind; only, in this case, the material objects are not pieces of metal, but marks made on white paper. Which is why a certain scientist was able to say: "My pencil knows more than I do."

It is obvious, of course, that higher mathematics are not a pure product of automatism, and that mind and even genius have played and play a part in their elaboration; the result is an extraordinary mixture of blind operations coupled with flashes of understanding; but where the mind cannot embrace everything, it must necessarily play a subordinate role. And the more scientific progress accumulates readymade combinations of signs, the more the mind is weighed down, made powerless to draw up an inventory of the ideas which it handles. Of course, the connection between the formulas thus worked out and the practical applications of them is often itself, too, completely impenetrable to the mind, with the result that it appears as fortuitous as the efficacy of a magic formula. In such a case work finds itself automatic, as it were, to the second power; it is not simply the execution, it is also the elaboration of the method of work which takes place outside the control of the mind. One might conceive, as an abstract limit, of a civilization in which all human activity, in the sphere of labour as in that of speculative theory, was subjected right down to matters of detail to an altogether mathematical strictness, and that without a single human being understanding anything at all about what he was doing; the idea of necessity would then be absent from everybody's mind, and in far more radical fashion than it is among primitive tribes which, our sociologists affirm, are ignorant of logic.

As opposed to this, the only mode of production absolutely free would be that in which methodical thought was in operation throughout the course of the work. The difficulties to be overcome would have to be so varied that it would never be possible to apply ready-made rules; not of course that the part played by acquired knowledge should be nil; but it is necessary that the worker should be obliged always to bear in mind the guiding principle behind the work in hand, so as to be able to apply it intelligently to ever-new sets of circumstances. The condition naturally governing such a presence of mind is that the fluidity of the body produced by habit and skill should reach a very high degree. All the ideas employed in the course of the work must also be sufficiently luminous to be able to be called up in their entirety in the twinkling of an eye; whether the memory is capable of retaining the idea itself or simply the formula that served to enshrine it depends on a greater or lesser adaptability of mind, but even more on the more or less direct means whereby an idea has taken shape in the mind. Furthermore, it goes without saying that the degree of complexity of the difficulties to be solved must never be too great, on pain of bringing about a split between thought and action. Naturally, such an ideal can never be fully realized; one cannot avoid, in the practical affairs of life, carrying out actions which it is impossible to understand at the moment when they are being carried out, because one has to rely either on ready-made rules or else on instinct, trial and error, routine. But one can at any rate widen bit by bit the sphere of conscious work, and perhaps indefinitely so. To achieve this end it would be enough if man were no longer to aim at extending his knowledge and power indefinitely, but rather at establishing, both in his research and in his work, a certain balance between the mind and the object to which it is being applied.

But there is still another factor making for servitude; it is, in the case of each man, the existence of other men. And indeed, when we look into it more closely, it is, strictly speaking, the only factor; man alone can enslave man. Even primitive men would not be the slaves of nature if they did not people her with imaginary beings comparable to man, whose wills are, furthermore, interpreted by men. In this case, as in all the others, it is the outside world that is the source of power; but if behind the infinite forces of nature there did not lie, whether as a result of fiction or in reality, divine or human wills, nature could break man, but she could not humiliate him. Matter can give the lie to expectations and ruin efforts, it remains none the less inert, made to be understood and handled from the outside; but the human mind can never be understood or handled from the outside. To the extent to which a man's fate is dependent on other men, his own life escapes not only out of his hands, but also out of the control of his intelligence; judgment and resolution no longer have anything to which to apply themselves; instead of contriving and acting, one has to stoop to pleading or threatening; and the soul is plunged into bottomless abysses of desire and fear, for there are no bounds to the satisfactions and sufferings that a man can receive at the hands of other men. This degrading dependence is not the characteristic of the oppressed only; it is for the same reason, though in different ways, that of both the oppressed and the powerful. As the man of power lives only by his slaves, the existence of an inexorable world escapes him almost entirely; his orders seem to him to contain within themselves some mysterious efficacy; he is never capable, strictly speaking, of willing, but is a prey to desires to which the clear perception of necessity never comes to assign any limit. Since he cannot conceive of any other mode of action than that of commanding, when he happens, as he inevitably does, to issue commands in vain, he passes all of a sudden from the feeling of absolute power to that of utter impotence, as often happens in dreams; and his fears are then all the more overwhelming in that he feels himself continually threatened by his rivals. As for the slaves, they are continually striving with material elements; only their lot does not depend on these material elements which they handle, but on masters whose whims are unaccountable and insatiable.

But it would still be a small matter to be dependent on other beings who, although strangers, are at any rate real and whom one can, if not penetrate, at least see, hear, divine by analogy with oneself. Actually, in all oppressive societies, any man, whatever his rank may be, is dependent not only on those above or below him, but above all on the very play of collective life—a blind play which alone determines the social hierarchies; and it does not matter much in this respect whether power allows its essentially collective origin to appear or else seems to reside in certain specific individuals after the manner of the dormitive virtue in opium. Now, if there is one thing in the world which is completely abstract, wholly mysterious, inaccessible to the senses and to the mind, it is the collectivity; the individual who is a member of it cannot, it would seem, reach up to or lay hold of it by any artifice, bring his weight to bear on it by the use of any lever; with respect to it he feels himself to be something infinitely small. If an individual's caprices seem arbitrary to everybody else, the shocks produced by collective life seem to be so to the second power. Thus between man and this universe which is assigned to him by destiny as the sole matter of his thoughts and actions, the relation oppression-servitude permanently sets the impenetrable screen of human arbitrariness. Why be surprised, then, if instead of ideas one encounters little but opinions, instead of action a blind agitation? One could only visualize the possibility of any progress in the true sense of the word, that is to say progress in the order of human values, if one could conceive as an ideal limit a society which armed man against the world without separating him from it.

Man is not made to be the plaything of the blind collectivities that he forms with his fellows, any more than he is made to be the plaything of a blind nature; but in order to cease being delivered over to society as passively as a drop of water is to the sea, he would have to be able both to understand and to act upon it. In all spheres, it is true, collective strength infinitely surpasses individual strength; thus you can no more easily conceive of an individual managing even a portion of the collective life than you can of a line extending itself by the addition of a point. Such, at any rate, is the appearance; but in reality there is one exception and one only, namely, the sphere of the mind. In the case of the mind, the relation is reversed; here the individual surpasses the collectivity to the same extent as something surpasses nothing, for thought only takes shape in a mind that is alone face to face with itself; collectivities do not think. It is true that mind by no means constitutes a force by itself. Archimedes was killed, so it is said, by a drunken soldier; and if he had been made to turn a millstone under the lash of a slave-overseer, he would have turned it in exactly the same manner as the most dull-witted man. To the extent to which the mind soars above the social *mêlée*, it can judge, but it cannot transform. All forms of force are material; the expression "spiritual force" is essentially contradictory; mind can only be a force to the extent to which it is materially indispensable. To express the same idea under another aspect, man has nothing essentially individual about him, nothing which is absolutely his own, apart from the faculty of thinking, and this society on which he is in close dependence every minute of his existence depends in its turn a little on him from the moment his thinking is necessary to it. For all the rest can be imposed from outside by force, including bodily movements, but nothing in the world can compel a man to exercise his powers of thought, nor take away from him the control over his own mind. If you require a slave to think, the lash had better be put away; otherwise you will run very little chance of obtaining high-quality results. Thus, if we wish to form, in a purely theoretical way, the conception of a society in which collective life would be subject to men as individuals instead of subjecting them to itself, we must visualize a form of material existence wherein only efforts exclusively directed by a clear intelligence would take place, which would imply that each worker himself had to control, without referring to any external rule, not only the adaptation of his efforts to the piece of work to be produced, but also their co-ordination with the efforts of all the other members of the collectivity. The technique would have to be such as to make continual use of methodical thought; the analogy between the techniques employed in the various tasks would have to be sufficiently close, and technical education sufficiently widespread, to enable each worker to form a clear idea of all the specialized procedures; co-ordination would have to be arranged in sufficiently simple a manner to enable each one continually to have a precise knowledge of it, as concerns both co-operation between workers and exchange of products; collectivities would never be sufficiently vast to pass outside the range of a human mind; community of interests would be sufficiently patent to abolish competitive attitudes; and as each individual would be in a position to exercise control over the collective life as a whole, the latter would always be in accordance with the general will. Privileges founded upon the exchange of products, secrets of production or co-ordination of labour would automatically be done away with. The function of co-ordinating would no longer imply power, since a continual check exercised by each individual would render any arbitrary decision impossible. Generally speaking, men's dependence with regard to one another would no longer imply that their fate rested in the hands of arbitrary factors, and would cease to introduce into human life any mysterious element whatever, since each would be in a position to verify the activities of all the rest by using his own reason. There is but one single and identical reason for all men; they only become estranged from and impenetrable to each other when they depart from it; thus a society in which the whole of material existence had as its necessary and sufficient condition that each individual should exercise his reason could be absolutely clearly understood by each individual mind. As for the stimulus necessary to overcome fatigue, sufferings and dangers, each would find it in the desire to win the esteem of his fellows, but even more so in himself; in the case of creative work by the mind, outward constraint, having become useless and harmful, is replaced by a sort of inward constraint; the sight of the unfinished task attracts the free man as powerfully as the over-seer's whip stimulates the slave. Such a society alone would be a society of men free, equal and brothers. Men would, it is true, be bound by collective ties, but exclusively in their capacity as men; they would never be treated by each other as things. Each would see in every work-fellow another self occupying another post, and would love him in the way that the Gospel maxim enjoins. Thus we should possess, over and above liberty, a still more precious good; for if nothing is more odious than the humiliation and degradation of man by man, nothing is so beautiful or so sweet as friendship.

The above picture, considered by itself, is, if possible, still farther removed from the actual conditions of human existence than is the fiction of a Golden Age. But, unlike that fiction, it is able to serve, by way of an ideal, as a standard for the analysis and evaluation of actual social patterns. The picture of a completely oppressive social life where every individual is subject to the operation of a blind mechanism was also purely theoretical; an analysis which situated a society with respect to these two pictures would already come much closer to reality, while still remaining very abstract. There thus emerges a new method of social analysis which is not that of Marx, although it starts, as Marx wanted, from the relationships of production; but whereas Marx,

whose conception is in any case not very precise on this point, seems to
have wanted to classify the modes of production in terms of output,
these would be analysed in terms of the relationships between thought
and action. It goes without saying that such a point of view in no way
implies that humanity has evolved, in the course of history, from the
least conscious to the most conscious forms of production; the idea of
progress is indispensable for whoever seeks to design the future in
advance, but it can only lead the mind astray when it is the past that is
being studied. We must then replace it by the idea of a scale of values
conceived outside time; but it is not possible, either, to arrange the
various social patterns in serial order according to such a scale. What
one can do is to refer to this scale such and such an aspect of social life,
taken at a given period.

It is clear enough that one kind of work differs substantially from
another by reason of something which has nothing to do with welfare,
or leisure, or security, and yet which claims each man's devotion; a
fisherman battling against wind and waves in his little boat, although
he suffers from cold, fatigue, lack of leisure and even of sleep, danger
and a primitive level of existence, has a more enviable lot than the
manual worker on a production-line, who is nevertheless better off as
regards nearly all these matters. That is because his work resembles far
more the work of a free man, despite the fact that routine and blind
improvisation sometimes play a fairly large part in it. The craftsman of
the Middle Ages also occupies, from this point of view, a fairly honour-
able position, although the "tricks of the trade" which play so large a
part in all work carried out by hand are to a great extent something
blind; as for the fully skilled worker, trained in modern technical
methods, he perhaps resembles most closely the perfect workman.

Similar differences are found in collective action; a team of workers
on a production-line under the eye of a foreman is a sorry spectacle,
whereas it is a fine sight to see a handful of workmen in the building
trade, checked by some difficulty, ponder the problem each for himself, make various suggestions for dealing with it, and then apply
unanimously the method conceived by one of them, who may or may
not have any official authority over the remainder. At such moments
the image of a free community appears almost in its purity. As for the
relationship between the nature of the work and the condition of the

worker, that, too, is clearly apparent, as soon as one takes a look at history or at our present-day society; even the slaves of antiquity were treated with consideration when they were employed as physicians or as pedagogues. However, all these remarks are still concerned only with details. A method enabling one to reach general views concerning the various modes of social organization in terms of the ideas of servitude and of liberty would be more valuable.

It would first of all be necessary to draw up something like a map of social life, a map indicating the spots where it is indispensable that thought should be exercised, and consequently, if one may so express it, the individual's zones of influence over society. It is possible to distinguish three ways in which thought can play a part in social life; it can formulate purely theoretical speculations, the results of which will afterwards be applied by technicians; it can be exercised in execution; it can be exercised in command and management. In all these cases, it is only a question of a partial and, as it were, maimed exercise of thought, since the mind is never able fully to embrace its object; but it is enough to ensure that those who are obliged to think when they are discharging their social function preserve the human aspect better than others. This is true not only for the oppressed, but also for all degrees of the social scale. In a society founded on oppression, it is not only the weak but also the most powerful who are bond-slaves to the blind demands of collective life, and in each case heart and mind suffer a diminution, though in different ways. If we compare two oppressive social strata such as, for example, the citizens of Athens and the Soviet bureaucracy, we find a distance between them at least as great as that between one of our skilled workmen and a Greek slave. As for the conditions under which thought plays a greater or lesser part in the exercise of power, it would be easy to tabulate them according to the degree of complexity and range of business, the general nature of the difficulties to be solved and the allocation of functions. Thus the members of an oppressive society are not only distinguished according to the higher or lower position in the social mechanism to which they cling, but also by the more conscious or more passive character of their relationship with it, and this second distinction—the more important of the two—has no direct connection with the first. As for the influence that men charged with social functions subject to the control of their own intelligence can exercise on the society of which they form a part, that depends, of course, on the nature and importance of these functions; it would be very interesting, but also very difficult, to carry out a detailed analysis with regard to this point.

Another very important factor in the relations between social oppression and individuals arises from the more or less extensive powers of control that can be exercised over the various functions essentially concerned in co-ordinating by men who are not themselves invested with such powers; it is obvious that the more these functions cannot be controlled, the more crushing collective life becomes for the general body of individuals. Finally, one must bear in mind the nature of the ties which keep the individual in material dependence upon the society surrounding him; at times these ties are looser, at other times tighter, and considerable differences may be found at this point, according to whether a man is more or less forced, at every moment of his existence, to address himself to others in order to have the where-withal to live, the wherewithal to produce, and to protect himself from outside danger. For example, a workman who has a large enough gar-den to supply himself with vegetables is more independent than those of his comrades who have to get all their food from the shopkeepers; an artisan who has his own tools is more independent than a factory worker whose hands become useless as soon as it pleases the boss to stop him from working his machine. As for protection against danger, the individual's position in this respect depends on the method of warfare practised by the society in which he finds himself; where fighting is the monopoly of those belonging to a certain social stratum, the security of everybody else depends on these privileged persons; where the destructive power of armaments and the collective nature of warfare give the central government the monopoly of military force, that government disposes of the security of the citizens as it likes. To sum up, the least evil society is that in which the general run of men are most often obliged to think while acting, have the most opportun-ities for exercising control over collective life as a whole, and enjoy the greatest amount of independence. Furthermore, the necessary condi-tions for diminishing the oppressive weight of the social mechanism run counter to each other as soon as certain limits are overstepped; thus the thing to do is not to proceed forward as far as possible in a specific direction, but, what is much more difficult, to discover a certain optimum balance.

The purely negative idea of a lessening of social oppression cannot by itself provide an objective for people of good will. It is indispensable to form at any rate a vague mental picture of the sort of civilization one wishes humanity to reach; and it matters little if this mental picture is derived more from mere reverie than from real thought. If the foregoing analyses are correct, the most fully human civilization would be that which had manual labour as its pivot, that in which manual labour constituted the supreme value. It is not a question of anything comparable to the religion of production which reigned in America during the period of prosperity, and has reigned in Russia since the Five Year Plan; for the true object of that religion is the product of work and not the worker, material objects and not man. It is not in relation to what it produces that manual labour must become the highest value, but in relation to the man who performs it; it must not be made the object of honours and rewards, but must constitute for each human being what he is most essentially in need of if his life is to take on of itself a meaning and a value in his own eyes. Even in these days, so-called disinterested activities, such as sport or even art or even thought, do not succeed in giving perhaps the equivalent of what one experiences in getting directly to grips with the world by means of non-mechanized labour. Rimbaud complained that "we are not in the world" and that "true life is absent"; in those moments of incomparable joy and fullness we know by flashes that true life is there at hand, we feel with all our being that the world exists and that we are in the world. Even physical fatigue cannot lessen the strength of this feeling, but rather, as long as it is not excessive, augments it. If this can be so in our day, what wonderful fullness of life could we not expect from a civilization in which labour would be sufficiently transformed to exercise fully all the faculties, to form the human act *par excellence*? It would then of necessity be at the very centre of culture. At one time culture was considered by many as an end in itself, and in our days those who see more in it than just a hobby usually look to it as a means of escape from real life. Its true value should consist, on the contrary, in preparing for real life, in equipping man so that he may maintain, both with this universe which is his portion and with his fellows whose condition is identical to his own, relations worthy of the greatness of humanity. Science is today regarded by some as a mere catalogue of technical recipes, by others as a body of pure intellectual speculations which are sufficient unto themselves; the former set too little value on the intellect, the latter on the world. Thought is certainly man's supreme dignity; but it is exercised in a vacuum, and consequently only in appearance, when it does not seize hold of its object, which can be none other than the universe. Now what gives the abstract speculations of the scientists that connection with the universe which alone can invest them with a concrete value, is the fact that they are directly or indirectly applicable. In our days, it is true, their own applications remain unknown to them; while those who elaborate or study those speculations do so without considering their theoretical value. At least that is more often than not the case. On the day when it became impossible to understand scientific notions, even the most abstract, without clearly perceiving at the same time their connection with possible applications, and equally impossible to apply such notions even indirectly without thoroughly knowing and understanding them—on that day science would have become concrete and labour would have become conscious; and then only will each possess its full value.

Until that time comes, there will always be something incomplete and inhuman about science and labour. Those who have so far maintained that applications are the goal of science meant to say that truth is not worth seeking and that success alone counts; but it could be understood differently; one can conceive of a science whose ultimate aim would be the perfecting of technique not by rendering it more powerful, but simply more conscious and more methodical. Besides, output might well increase in proportion with clear thinking; "seek ye first the kingdom of God . . . and all these things shall be added unto you". Such a science would be, in effect, a method for mastering nature, or a catalogue of concepts indispensable for attaining to such mastery, arranged according to an order that would make them palpably clear to the mind. Presumably Descartes conceived science after this fashion. As for the art of such a civilization, it would crystallize in its works the expression of that happy balance between mind and body, between man and the universe, which can exist in action only in the noblest forms of physical labour; moreover, even in the past, the purest works of art have always expressed the sentiment, or, to speak perhaps with greater precision, the presentiment of such a balance. The essential aim of sport would be to give the human body that suppleness and, as Hegel says, that fluidity which renders it pervious to thought and enables the latter to enter directly into contact with material objects. Social relations would be directly modelled upon the organization of labour; men would group themselves in small working collectivities, where co-operation would be the sovereign law, and where each would be able to understand clearly and to verify the connection between the rules to which his life was subjected and the public interest. Moreover, every moment of existence would afford each the opportunity to understand and to feel how profoundly all men are one, since they all have to bring one same reason to bear on similar obstacles; and all human relations, from the most superficial to the very tenderest, would have about them something of that manly and brotherly feeling which forms the bond between workmates.

No doubt all this is purely utopian. But to give even a summary description of a state of things which would be better than what actually exists is always to build a utopia; yet nothing is more necessary to our life than such descriptions, provided it is always reason that is responsible for them. The whole of modern thought since the Renaissance is, moreover, impregnated with more or less vague aspirations towards such a utopian civilization; for some time it was even thought that this civilization was beginning to take shape, and that men were entering upon a period when Greek geometry would descend upon earth. Descartes certainly believed this, as also did some of his contemporaries. Furthermore, the idea of labour considered as a human value is doubtless the one and only spiritual conquest achieved by the human mind since the miracle of Greece; this was perhaps the only gap in the ideal of human life elaborated by Greece and left behind by her as an undying heritage. Bacon was the first to put forward this idea. For the ancient and heart-breaking curse contained in Genesis, which made the world appear as a convict prison and labour as the sign of men's servitude and abasement, he substituted in a flash of genius the veritable charter expressing the relations between man and the world: "We cannot command Nature except by obeying her." This simple pronouncement ought to form by itself the Bible of our times. It suffices to define true labour, the kind which forms free men, and that to the very extent to which it is an act of conscious submission to necessity. After Descartes, scientists progressively slipped into considering pure science as an end in itself; but the ideal of a life devoted to some free form of physical labour began, on the other hand, to be perceived by writers; and it even dominates the masterpiece of the poet usually regarded as the most aristocratic of all, namely, Goethe. Faust, a symbol of the human soul in its untiring pursuit of the good, abandons with disgust the abstract search for truth, which has become in his eyes an empty and barren occupation; love merely leads him to destroy the loved one; political and military power reveals itself as nothing but a game of appearances; the meeting with beauty fulfils his dreams, but only for the space of a second; his position as industrial leader gives him a power which he believes to be substantial, but which nevertheless delivers him up to the tyranny of the passions. Finally, he longs to be stripped of his magic power, which can be regarded as the symbol of all forms of power, and he exclaims: "If I could stand before thee, Nature, simply as a man, then it would be worth while being a human creature"; and he ends by having, at the moment of death, a foretaste of the most complete happiness, by representing to himself a life spent freely among a free people and entirely taken up by hard and dangerous physical labour, which would, however, be carried out in the midst of brotherly co-operation. It would be easy to cite yet other famous names, amongst them Rousseau, Shelley and, above all, Tolstoy, who developed this theme throughout the whole of his work in matchless accents. As for the working-class movement, every time it has managed to escape from demagogy, it is on the dignity of labour that it has based the workers' demands. Proudhon dared to write: "The genius of the humblest artisan is as much superior to the materials with which he works as is the mind of a Newton to the lifeless spheres whose distances, masses and revolutions he calculates." Marx, whose work contains a good many contradictions, set down as man's essential characteristic, as opposed to the animals, the fact that he produces the conditions of his own existence and thus himself indirectly produces himself. The revolutionary syndicalists, who place at the core of the social problem the dignity of the producer as such, are linked up with the same current of ideas. On the whole, we may feel proud to belong to a civilization which has brought with it the presage of a new ideal.

SKETCH OF CONTEMPORARY SOCIAL LIFE

It is impossible to imagine anything more contrary to this ideal than the form which modern civilization has assumed in our day, at the end of a development lasting several centuries. Never has the individual been so completely delivered up to a blind collectivity, and never have men been less capable, not only of subordinating their actions to their thoughts, but even of thinking. Such terms as oppressors and oppressed, the idea of classes—all that sort of thing is near to losing all meaning, so obvious are the impotence and distress of all men in face of the social machine, which has become a machine for breaking hearts and crushing spirits, a machine for manufacturing irresponsibility, stupidity, corruption, slackness and, above all, dizziness. The reason for this painful state of affairs is perfectly clear. We are living in a world in which nothing is made to man's measure; there exists a monstrous discrepancy between man's body, man's mind and the things which at the present time constitute the elements of human existence; everything is disequilibrium. There is not a single category, group or class of men that is altogether exempt from this destructive disequilibrium, except perhaps for a few isolated patches of more primitive life; and the younger generation, who have grown and are growing up in it, inwardly reflect the chaos surrounding them more than do their elders. This disequilibrium is essentially a matter of quantity. Quantity is changed into quality, as Hegel said, and in particular a mere difference in quantity is sufficient to change what is human into what is inhuman. From the abstract point of view quantities are immaterial, since you can arbitrarily change the unit of measurement; but from the concrete point of view certain units of measurement are given and have hitherto remained invariable, such as the human body, human life, the year, the day, the average quickness of human thought. Present-day life is not organized on the scale of all these things; it has been transported into an altogether different order of magnitude, as though man were trying to raise it to the level of the forces of outside nature while neglecting to take his own nature into account. If we add

Th

EX, ...

a) M P   b) Cog. Fac.
              much more surveil
              in cold world

- how to get warrant   a) P F
- all. to Finds Prison Gallof   b) C E
lacks A T B, Marx makes it   c) A T G
lacks P F us vrm Bg 2 9   U) S A T G

that, to all appearances, the economic system has exhausted its constructive capacity and is beginning to be able to function only by undermining little by little its own material foundations, we shall perceive in all its simplicity the veritable essence of the bottomless misery that forms the lot of the present generations.

In appearance, nearly everything nowadays is carried out methodically; science is king, machinery invades bit by bit the entire field of labour, statistics take on a growing importance, and over one-sixth of the globe the central authority is trying to regulate the whole of social life according to plans. But in reality methodical thought is progressively disappearing, owing to the fact that the mind finds less and less matter on which to bite. Mathematics by itself forms too vast and too complex a whole to be embraced by one mind; *a fortiori* the whole formed by mathematics and the natural sciences; *a fortiori* the whole formed by science and its applications; and, on the other hand, everything is too intimately connected for the mind to be able really to grasp partial concepts. Now everything that the individual becomes powerless to control is seized upon by the collectivity. Thus science has now been for a long time—and to an ever-increasing extent—a collective enterprise. Actually, new results are always, in fact, the work of specific individuals; but, save perhaps for rare exceptions, the value of any result depends on such a complex set of interrelations with past discoveries and possible future researches that even the mind of the inventor cannot embrace the whole. Consequently, new discoveries, as they go on accumulating, take on the appearance of enigmas, after the style of too thick a glass which ceases to be transparent. *A fortiori* practical life takes on a more and more collective character, and the individual as such a more and more insignificant place in it. Technical progress and mass production reduce manual workers more and more to a passive role; in increasing proportion and to an ever greater extent they arrive at a form of labour that enables them to carry out the necessary movements without understanding their connection with the final result. On the other hand, an industrial concern has become something too vast and too complex for any one man to be able to grasp it fully; and furthermore, in all spheres, the men who occupy key posts in social life are in charge of matters which are far beyond the compass of any single human mind. As for the general body of social life, it depends on so many factors, each of which is impenetrably obscure and which are tangled up in inextricable relations with one another, that it would never even occur to anyone to try to understand its mechanism. Thus the social function most essentially connected with the individual, that which consists in co-ordinating, managing, deciding, is beyond any individual's capacity and becomes to a certain extent collective and, as it were, anonymous.

To the very extent to which what is systematic in contemporary life escapes the control of the mind, its regularity is established by things which constitute the equivalent of what collective thought would be if the collectivity did think. The cohesiveness of science is ensured by means of signs; namely, on the one hand, by words or ready-made phrases whose use is stretched beyond the meanings originally contained in them, on the other hand, by algebraic calculations. In the sphere of labour, the things which take upon themselves the essential functions are machines. The thing which relates production to consumption and governs the exchange of products is money. Finally, where the function of co-ordination and management is too heavy for the mind and intelligence of one man, it is entrusted to a curious machine, whose parts are men, whose gears consist of regulations, reports and statistics, and which is called bureaucratic organization. All these blind things imitate the effort of thought to the life. Just the mechanism of algebraic calculation has led more than once to what might be called a new idea, except that the content of such pseudo-ideas is no more than that of relations between signs; and algebra is often marvellously apt to transform a series of experimental results into laws, with a disconcerting ease reminding one of the fantastic transformations one sees in motion-picture cartoons. Automatic machines seem to offer the model for the intelligent, faithful, docile and conscientious worker. As for money, economists have long been convinced that it possesses the virtue of establishing harmonious relations between the various economic functions. And bureaucratic machines almost reach the point of taking the place of leaders. Thus, in all spheres, thought, the prerogative of the individual, is subordinated to vast mechanisms which crystallize collective life, and that is so to such an extent that we have almost lost the notion of what real thought is. The efforts, the labours, the inventions of beings of flesh and blood whom time introduces in successive waves to social life only possess social value and effectiveness on condition that they become in their turn crystallized in these huge mechanisms. The inversion of the relation between means and ends—an inversion which is to a certain extent the law of every oppressive society—here becomes total or nearly so, and extends to nearly everything. The scientist does not use science in order to manage to see more clearly into his own thinking, but aims at discovering results that will go to swell the present volume of scientific knowledge. Machines do not run in order to enable men to live, but we resign ourselves to feeding men in order that they may serve the machines. Money does not provide a convenient method for exchanging products; it is the sale of goods which is a means for keeping money in circulation. Lastly, organization is not a means for exercising a collective activity, but the activity of a group, whatever it may be, is a means for strengthening organization. Another aspect of the same inversion consists in the fact that signs, words and algebraic formulas in the field of knowledge, money and credit symbols in economic life, play the part of realities of which the actual things themselves constitute only the shadows, exactly as in Hans Andersen's tale in which the scientist and his shadow exchanged roles; this is because signs constitute the material of social relations, whereas the perception of reality is something individual. The dispossession of the individual in favour of the collectivity is not, indeed, absolute, and it cannot become so; but it is hard to imagine how it could go much farther than at present. The power and concentration of armaments place all human lives at the mercy of the central authority. As a result of the vast extension of exchange, the majority of men cannot procure for themselves the greater part of what they consume save through the medium of society and in return for money; the peasants themselves are today to a large extent under this obligation to buy. And as big industry is a system of collective production, a great many men are forced, in order that their hands may come into contact with the material of work, to go through a collectivity which swallows them up and pins them down to a more or less servile task; when it rejects them, the strength and skill of their hands remain useless. The very peasants, who hitherto had managed to escape this wretched condition, have been reduced to it of late over one-sixth of the globe. Such a stifling state of affairs certainly provokes here and there an individualistic reaction; art, and especially literature, bears the marks of it; but since, owing to objective conditions, this reaction cannot impinge on either the sphere of thought or that of action, it remains bottled up in the play of the inner consciousness or in dreams of adventure and gratuitous acts, in other words, it never leaves the realm of shadows; and everything leads one to suppose that even this shadowy reaction is doomed to disappear almost completely.

When man reaches this degree of enslavement, judgments of value can only be based, whatever the particular field may be, on a purely external criterion; language does not possess any term so foreign to thought as properly to express something so devoid of meaning; but we may say that this criterion is constituted by efficiency, provided we thereby understand successes obtained in a vacuum. Even a scientific concept is not valued according to its content, which may be completely unintelligible, but according to the opportunities it provides for co-ordinating, abbreviating, summarizing. In the economic field, an undertaking is judged, not according to the real utility of the social functions it fulfils, but according to its growth so far and the speed with which it is developing; and the same is true of everything. Thus judgment of values is as it were entrusted to material objects instead of to the mind. The efficacy of efforts of whatever kind must always, it is true, be verified by thought, for, generally speaking, all verification proceeds from the mind; but thought has been reduced to such a subordinate role that one may say, by way of simplification, that the function of verification has passed from thought to things. But this excessive complication of all theoretical and practical activities which has thus dethroned thought, finally, when still further aggravated, comes to render the verification exercised by things in its turn imperfect and almost impossible. Everything is then blind. Thus it is that, in the sphere of science, the excessive accumulation of materials of every kind produces such chaos that the time seems to be approaching when any system will appear arbitrary. The chaos existing in economic life is still far more patent. In the actual carrying out of work, the subordination of irresponsible slaves to leaders overwhelmed by the mass of things to attend to, and, incidentally, themselves to a large extent irresponsible, is the cause of faulty workmanship and countless acts of negligence; this evil, which was first of all restricted to the big industrial undertakings, has now spread to the countryside wherever the peasants are enslaved after the manner of the industrial workers, that is to say, in Soviet Russia. The tremendous extension of credit prevents money from playing its regulating role so far as concerns commercial exchanges and the relationships between the various branches of production; and it would be useless to try to remedy this by doses of statistics. The parallel extension of speculation ends up by rendering the prosperity of industries independent, to a large extent, of their good functioning; the reason being that the capital increase brought about by the actual production of each of them counts less and less as compared with the constant supply of fresh capital. In short, in all spheres, success has become something almost arbitrary; it seems more and more to be the work of pure chance; and as it constituted the sole rule in all branches of human activity, our civilization is invaded by an ever-increasing disorder, and ruined by a waste in proportion to that disorder. This transformation is taking place at the very moment when the sources of profit on which the capitalist economy formerly drew for its prodigious development are becoming less and less plentiful, and when the technical conditions of work are themselves imposing a rapidly decreasing tempo on the improvement of industrial equipment.

So many profound changes have been taking place almost unbeknownst to us, and yet we are living in a period when the very axis of the social system is as it were in process of heeling over. Throughout the rise of the industrial system social life found itself oriented in the direction of construction. The industrial equipment of the planet was the supreme battle-ground on which the struggle for power was waged. To increase the size of an undertaking faster than its competitors, and that by means of its own resources—such was, broadly speaking, the aim and object of economic activity. Saving was the rule of economic life; consumption was restricted as much as possible, not only that of the workers, but also that of the capitalists themselves, and, in general, all expenditure connected with other things than industrial equipment. The supreme mission of governments was to preserve peace at home and abroad. The bourgeoisie were under the impression that this state of things would go on indefinitely, for the greater happiness of humanity; but it could not go on indefinitely in this way. Nowadays, the struggle for power, while preserving to a certain extent the same outward appearance, has entirely changed in character. The formidable increase in the part capital plant plays in undertakings, if compared with that of living labour, the rapid decrease in the rate of profit which has resulted, the ever-increasing amount of overhead expenses, waste, leakage, the lack of any regulating device for adjusting the various branches of production to one another—everything prevents social activity from still having as its pivot the development of the undertaking by turning profits into capital. It seems as though the economic struggle has ceased to be a form of competition in order to become a sort of war. It is no longer so much a question of properly organizing the work as of squeezing out the greatest possible amount of available capital scattered about in society by marketing shares, and then of squeezing out the greatest possible amount of money from everywhere by marketing products; everything takes place in the realm of opinion, and almost of fiction, by means of speculation and publicity. Since credit is the key to all economic success, saving is replaced by the maddest forms of expenditure. The term property has almost ceased to have any meaning; the ambitious man no longer thinks of being owner of a business and running it at a profit, but of causing the widest possible sector of economic activity to pass under his control. In a word, if we attempt to characterize, albeit in vague and summary fashion, this almost impenetrably obscure transformation, it is now a question in the struggle for economic power far less of building up than of conquering; and since conquest is destructive, the capitalist system, though remaining outwardly pretty much the same as it was fifty years ago, is wholly turned towards destruction. The means employed in the economic struggle—publicity, lavish display of wealth, corruption, enormous capital investments based almost entirely on credit, marketing of useless products by almost violent methods, speculations with the object of ruining rival concerns—all these tend to undermine the foundations of our economic life far more than to broaden them.

But all that is little enough compared with two related phenomena which are beginning to appear clearly and to cause a tragic threat to weigh upon the life of everyone; namely, on the one hand, the fact that the State tends more and more, and with an extraordinary rapidity, to become the centre of economic and social life, and, on the other hand, the subordination of economic to military interests. If one tries to analyse these phenomena in detail, one is held up by an almost inextricable web of reciprocal causes and effects; but the general trend is clear enough. It is quite natural that the increasingly bureaucratic nature of economic activity should favour the development of the power of the State, which is the bureaucratic organization *par excellence*. The profound change in the economic struggle operates in the same direction; the State is incapable of constructing, but owing to the fact that it concentrates in its hands the most powerful means of coercion, it is brought, as it were, by its very weight gradually to become the central element when it comes to conquering and destroying. Finally, seeing that the extraordinary complication of exchange and credit operations prevents money henceforth from sufficing to co-ordinate economic life, a semblance of bureaucratic co-ordination has to make up for it; and the central bureaucratic organization, which is the State machine, must naturally be led sooner or later to take the main hand in this co-ordination. The pivot around which revolves social life, thus transformed, is none other than preparation for war. Seeing that the struggle for power is carried out by conquest and destruction, in other words by a diffused economic war, it is not surprising that actual war should come to occupy the foreground. And since war is the recognized form of the struggle for power when the competitors are States, every increase in the State's grip on economic life has the effect of orienting industrial life yet a little farther towards preparation for war; while, conversely, the ever-increasing demands occasioned by preparation for war help day by day to bring the all-round economic and social activities of each country more and more into subjection to the authority of the central power. It seems fairly clear that contemporary humanity tends pretty well everywhere towards a totalitarian form of social organization—to use the term which the national-socialists have made fashionable—that is to say, towards a system in which the State power comes to exercise sovereign sway in all spheres, even, indeed above all, in that of thought. Russia presents us with an almost perfect example of such a system, for the greater misfortune of the Russian people; other countries will only be able to approach it, short of upheavals similar to that of October 1917; but it seems inevitable that all of them will approach it more or less in the course of the coming years. This development will only give disorder a bureaucratic form, and still further increase confusion, waste and misery. Wars will bring in their train a frantic consumption of raw materials and capital equipment, a crazy destruction of wealth of all kinds that previous generations have bequeathed us. When chaos and destruction have reached the limit beyond which the very functioning of the economic and social organization becomes materially impossible, our civilization will perish; and humanity, having gone back to a more or less primitive level of existence and to a social life dispersed into much smaller collectivities, will set out again along a new road which it is quite impossible for us to predict.

To imagine that we can switch the course of history along a different track by transforming the system through reforms or revolutions, to hope to find salvation in a defensive or offensive action against tyranny and militarism—all that is just day-dreaming. There is nothing on which to base even attempts. Marx's assertion that the régime would produce its own gravediggers is cruelly contradicted every day; and one wonders, incidentally, how Marx could ever have believed that slavery could produce free men. Never yet in history has a régime of slavery fallen under the blows of the slaves. The truth is that, to quote a famous saying, slavery degrades man to the point of making him love it; that liberty is precious only in the eyes of those who effectively possess it; and that a completely inhuman system, as ours is, far from producing beings capable of building up a human society, models all those subjected to it—oppressed and oppressors alike—according to its own image. Everywhere, in varying degrees, the impossibility of relating what one gives to what one receives has killed the feeling for sound workmanship, the sense of responsibility, and has developed passivity, neglect, the habit of expecting everything from outside, the belief in miracles. Even in the country, the feeling of a deep-seated bond between the land which sustains the man and the man who works the land has to a large extent been obliterated since the taste for speculation, the unpredictable rises and falls in currencies and prices have got countryfolk into the habit of turning their eyes towards the towns. The worker has not the feeling of earning his living as a producer; it is merely that the undertaking keeps him enslaved for long hours every day and allows him each week a sum of money which gives him the magic power of conjuring up at a moment's notice ready-made products, exactly as the rich do. The presence of innumerable unemployed, the cruel necessity of having to beg for a job, make wages appear less as wages than as alms. As for the unemployed themselves, the fact that they are involuntary parasites, and poverty-stricken into the bargain, does not make them any the less parasites. Generally speaking, the relation between work done and money earned is so hard to grasp that it appears as almost accidental, so that labour takes on the aspect of servitude, money that of a favour. The so-called governing classes are affected by the same passivity as all the others, owing to the fact that, snowed under as they are by an avalanche of inextricable problems, they long since gave up governing. One would look in vain, from the highest down to the lowest rungs of the social ladder, for a class of men among whom the idea could one day spring up that they might, in certain circumstances, have to take in hand the destinies of society; the harangues of the fascists could alone give the illusion of this, but they are empty.

As always happens, mental confusion and passivity leave free scope to the imagination On all hands one is obsessed by a representation of social life which, while differing considerably from one class to another, is always made up of mysteries, occult qualities, myths, idols and monsters; each one thinks that power resides mysteriously in one of the classes to which he has no access, because hardly anybody understands that it resides nowhere, so that the dominant feeling everywhere is that dizzy fear which is always brought about by loss of contact with reality. Each class appears from the outside as a nightmare object. In circles connected with the working-class movement, dreams are haunted by mythological monsters called Finance, Industry, Stock Exchange, Bank, etc.; the bourgeois dream about other monsters which they call ringleaders, agitators, demagogues; the politicians regard the capitalists as supernatural beings who alone possess the key to the situation, and *vice versa*; each nation regards its neighbours as collective monsters inspired by a diabolical perversity. One could go on developing this theme indefinitely. In such a situation, any log whatever can be looked upon as king and take the place of one up to a certain point thanks to that belief alone; and this is true, not merely in the case of men in general, but also in that of the governing classes. Nothing is easier, for that matter, than to spread any myth whatsoever throughout a whole population. We must not be surprised, therefore, at the appearance of "totalitarian" régimes unprecedented in history. It is often said that force is powerless to overcome thought; but for this to be true, there must be thought. Where irrational opinions hold the place of ideas, force is all-powerful. It is quite unfair to say, for example, that fascism annihilates free thought; in reality it is the lack of free thought which makes it possible to impose by force official doctrines entirely devoid of meaning. Actually, such a régime even manages considerably to increase the general stupidity, and there is little hope for the generations that will have grown up under the conditions which it creates. Nowadays, every attempt to turn men into brutes finds powerful means at its disposal. On the other hand, one thing is impossible, even were you to dispose of the best of public platforms, and that is to diffuse clear ideas, correct reasoning and sensible views on any wide scale.

It is no good expecting help to come from men; and even were it otherwise, men would none the less be vanquished in advance by the natural power of things. The present social system provides no means of action other than machines for crushing humanity; whatever may be the intentions of those who use them, these machines crush and will continue to crush as long as they exist. With the industrial convict prisons constituted by the big factories, one can only produce slaves and not free workers, still less workers who would form a dominant class. With guns, aeroplanes, bombs, you can spread death, terror, oppression, but not life and liberty. With gas masks, air-raid shelters and air-raid warnings, you can create wretched masses of panic-stricken human beings, ready to succumb to the most senseless forms of terror and to welcome with gratitude the most humiliating forms of tyranny, but not citizens. With the popular press and the wireless, you can make a whole people swallow with their breakfast or their supper a series of ready-made and, by the same token, absurd opinions—for even sensible views become deformed and falsified in minds which accept them unthinkingly; but you cannot with the aid of these things arouse so much as a gleam of thought. And without factories, without arms, without the popular press you can do nothing against those who possess all these things. The same applies to everything. The powerful means are oppressive, the non-powerful means remain inoperative. Each time that the oppressed have tried to set up groups able to exercise a real influence, such groups, whether they went by the name of parties or unions, have reproduced in full within themselves all the vices of the system which they claimed to reform or abolish, namely, bureaucratic organization, reversal of the relationship between means and ends, contempt for the individual, separation between thought and action, the mechanization of thought itself, the exploitation of stupidity and lies as means of propaganda, and so on.

The only possibility of salvation would lie in a methodical co-operation between all, strong and weak, with a view to accomplishing a progressive decentralization of social life; but the absurdity of such an idea strikes one immediately. Such a form of co-operation is impossible to imagine, even in dreams, in a civilization that is based on competition, on struggle, on war. Apart from some such co-operation, there is no means of stopping the blind trend of the social machine towards an increasing centralization, until the machine itself suddenly jams and flies into pieces. What weight can the hopes and desires of those who are not at the control levers carry, when, reduced to the most tragic impotence, they find themselves the mere playthings of blind and brutish forces As for those who exercise economic or political authority, harried as they are incessantly by rival ambitions and hostile powers, they cannot work to weaken their own authority without condemning themselves almost certainly to being deprived of it. The more they feel themselves to be animated by good intentions, the more they will be brought, even despite themselves, to endeavour to extend their authority in order to increase their ability to do good; which amounts to oppressing people in the hope of liberating them, as Lenin did. It is quite patently impossible for decentralization to be initiated by the central authority; to the very extent to which the central authority is exercised, it brings everything else under its subjection. Generally speaking, the idea of enlightened despotism, which has always had a utopian flavour about it, is in our day completely absurd. Faced with problems whose variety and complexity are infinitely beyond the range of great as of limited minds, no despot in the world can possibly be enlightened. Though a few men may hope, by dint of honest and methodical thinking, to perceive a few gleams in this impenetrable darkness, those whom the cares and responsibilities of authority deprive of both leisure and liberty of mind are certainly not of that number.

In such a situation, what can those do who still persist, against all eventualities, in honouring human dignity both in themselves and in others? Nothing, except endeavour to introduce a little play into the cogs of the machine that is grinding us down; seize every opportunity of awakening a little thought wherever they are able; encourage whatever is capable, in the sphere of politics, economics or technique, of leaving the individual here and there a certain freedom of movement amid the trammels cast around him by the social organization. That is certainly something, but it does not go very far. On the whole, our present situation more or less resembles that of a party of absolutely ignorant travellers who find themselves in a motor-car launched at full speed and driverless across broken country. When will the smash-up occur after which it will be possible to consider trying to construct something new? Perhaps it is a matter of a few decades, perhaps of centuries. There are no data enabling one to fix a probable lapse of time. It seems, however, that the material resources of our civilization are not likely to become exhausted for some considerable time, even allowing for wars; and, on the other hand, as centralization, by abolishing all individual initiative and all local life, destroys by its very existence everything which might serve as a basis for a different form of organization, one may suppose that the present system will go on existing up to the extreme limit of possibility. To sum up, it seems reasonable to suppose that the generations which will have to face the difficulties brought about by the collapse of the present system have yet to be born. As for the generations now living, they are perhaps, of all those that have followed each other in the course of human history, the ones which will have had to shoulder the maximum of imaginary responsibilities and the minimum of real ones. Once this situation is fully realized, it leaves a marvellous freedom of mind.

CONCLUSION

What exactly will perish and what subsist of our present civiization? What are the conditions and what is the direction in which history will afterwards unfold itself? These questions are insoluble. What we know in advance is that life will be proportionately less inhuman according as the individual ability to think and act is greater. Our present civilization, of which our descendents will no doubt inherit some fragments, at any rate contains, we feel it only too keenly, the wherewithal to crush man; but it also contains, at least in germ, the wherewithal to liberate him. Our science includes, despite all the obscurities engendered by a sort of new scholasticism, some admirable flashes of genius, some parts that are clear and luminous, some perfectly methodical steps undertaken by the mind. In our technique also the germs of a liberation of labour can be found: probably not, as is commonly thought, in the direction of automatic machines; these certainly appear to be suitable, from the purely technical point of view, for relieving men of the mechanical and unconscious element contained in labour, but, on the other hand, they are indissolubly bound up with an excessively centralized and consequently very oppressive economic organization. But other forms of the machine-tool have produced—above all before the war—perhaps the finest type of conscious worker history has ever seen, namely, the skilled workman. If, in the course of the last twenty years, the machine-tool has become more and more automatic in its functioning, if the work carried out, even on machines of relatively ancient design, has become more and more mechanical, the reason lies in the ever-increasing concentration of the economy. Who knows whether an industry split up into innumerable small undertakings would not bring about an inverse development of the machine-tool, and, at the same time, types of work calling for a yet greater consciousness and ingenuity than the most highly skilled work in modern factories? We are all the more justified in entertaining such hopes in that electricity supplies the form of energy suitable for such a type of industrial organization.

Given that once we have fully realized our almost complete powerlessness in regard to present-day ills we are at any rate relieved of the duty of concerning ourselves with the present state of things, apart from those moments when we feel its direct impact, what nobler task could we assume than that of preparing for such a future in a methodical way by devoting ourselves to drawing up an inventory of modern civilization? It is certainly a task which goes far beyond the narrow possibilities of a single human life; on the other hand, to pursue such a course is to condemn oneself of a certainty to moral loneliness, to lack of understanding, to the hostility of the enemies as well as of the servants of the existing order. As for future generations, nothing entitles us to assume that, across the upheavals which separate us from them, chance may allow the fragmentary ideas that might be elaborated by a few solitary minds in our day even to reach them. But it would be folly to complain of such a situation. No pact with Providence has ever guaranteed the effectiveness of even the most nobly-inspired efforts. And when one has resolved to place confidence, within and around oneself solely in efforts whose source and origin lie in the mind of the very person who accomplishes them, it would be foolish to wish that some magical operation should enable great results to be obtained with the insignificant forces placed at the disposal of isolated individuals. It is never by such arguments that a staunch mind can allow itself to be deflected, once it has clearly perceived that there is one thing to be done, and one only.

It would thus seem to be a question of separating, in present-day civilization, what belongs of right to man, considered as an individual, and what is of a nature to place weapons in the hands of the collectivity for use against him, whilst at the same time trying to discover the means whereby the former elements may be developed at the expense of the latter. As far as science is concerned, we must no longer seek to add to the already over-great mass which it forms; we must draw up its balance-sheet, so as to enable the mind to place in evidence there what is properly its own, what is made up of clear concepts, and to set aside what is only an automatic procedure for co-ordinating, unifying, summarizing or even discovering; we must try to reduce these procedures themselves to conscious steps on the part of the mind; we must, generally speaking, wherever possible, conceive of and present scientific results as merely a phase in the methodical activity of the mind. For this purpose, a serious study of the history of the sciences is probably indispensable. As for technique, it ought to be studied in a thoroughgoing manner—its history, present state, possibilities of development—and that from an entirely new point of view, which would no longer be that of output, but that of the relation between the worker and his work. Lastly, the analogy between the steps accomplished by the human mind, on the one hand in daily life and particularly in work, on the other hand in the methodical development of science, should be fully brought out. Even if a sequence of mental efforts oriented in this sense were to remain without influence on the future evolution of social organization, it would not lose its value on that account; the future destinies of humanity are not the sole object worthy of consideration. Only fanatics are able to set no value on their own existence save to the extent that it serves a collective cause; to react against the subordination of the individual to the collectivity implies that one begins by refusing to subordinate one's own destiny to the course of history. In order to resolve upon undertaking such an effort of critical analysis, all one needs is to realize that it would enable him who did so to escape the contagion of folly and collective frenzy by reaffirming on his own account, over the head of the social idol, the original pact between the mind and the universe.

(1934)

FRAGMENTS, 1933–1938

I

The situation in which we find ourselves is of an unprecedented gravity. The most progressive and best organized proletariat in the world has not only been vanquished, but has capitulated without resistance. This is the second time in twenty years. During the war, our elders could still hope that the Russian proletariat, by its magnificent uprising, was going to rouse the European workers. In our case, nothing entitles us to entertain similar hopes; there is no sign anywhere heralding some future victory capable of compensating for the crushing and unopposed defeat of the German workers. Never before, perhaps, since a working-class movement first started, has the relative balance of forces been so unfavourable to the proletariat as today, fifty years after the death of Marx.

What remains to us of Marx, fifty years after his death? His doctrine is indestructible; each one can seek it out in his works and assimilate it by thinking it out anew; and although, nowadays, a few barren formulas devoid of any real significance are hawked about under the name of Marxism, there are yet a few militants who go back to the source. But despite the fact that Marx's analyses possess a value that can never perish, the object of those analyses, namely, the society contemporary with Marx, no longer exists. Marxism can only remain something living on one condition, which is that the precious tool constituted by the Marxist method should come down from generation to generation without getting rusty, each generation making use of it in order to define the world in which it lives. This is what the pre-war generation understood, as Lenin's pamphlet on imperialism and a number of German publications show. All that is, unfortunately, very sketchy. But what have we, the post-war generation, done in this respect? Judging from the literature of the working-class movement, one would say that nothing new had turned up since Marx and Lenin. And yet there is, "over one-sixth of the globe", an economic régime whose like has never before been known or envisaged; in the rest of the world, paper money, inflation, the increasing role played by the State in the economy, rationalization and a host of other changes have come to modify, and possibly transform, economic relationships; for over four years we have been living through a crisis such as has never been known before. What do we know about all this As for myself, I cannot enumerate these questions without realizing, with a bitter feeling of shame, my own ignorance; and unfortunately there is not, as far as I know, anything in the literature of the working-class movement to entitle one to think that there are, at the present time, Marxists capable of resolving, or even of formulating clearly, the basic questions posed by the present economic set-up. That is why we must not be surprised if, fifty years after Marx's death, Marxists themselves in fact treat politics as though they formed a separate field, having little connection with the field of economic facts. In the communist daily press, the division into classes which, in Marx, was meant to explain political phenomena by relationships of production, has become the source of a new mythology; the bourgeoisie, in particular, plays in it the role of a mysterious and maleficent divinity, which brings about the phenomena that are necessary to its purposes, and whose desires and subterfuges explain almost everything that happens. More serious communist literature does not altogether escape such nonsense, and this is true even among the opposition groups, even in certain of Trotsky's analyses. And, of course, since the political conceptions are not based on economics and can no more progress in a vacuum than a bird could fly without air resistance, they are those that the years before and during the war have bequeathed us. The reformist tendency remains what it has always been; so does the anarchist ideology; revolutionary trade unionists dream about the old C.G.T.; orthodox and oppositional communists argue together as to which of them imitates more closely the Bolshevik party of before the war. All behave like beings deprived of consciousness as they go through this new period in which we are living, a period which cannot be defined by any of the analyses previously made, and in which it seems that only men's bodies are alive, while their minds are still moving in the pre-war world that has disappeared.

II

The question of the social structure can be reduced to that of classes.

Up to now, history has only shown us societies divided up into classes, except for altogether primitive societies in which no differentiation has yet occurred. As soon as production has become a little developed, society is split into various categories which oppose each other and whose interests are at variance. The most striking opposition is that which exists between non-producers and producers, or, in other words, between exploiters and exploited; for the non-producers necessarily consume what is produced by others, and consequently exploit them. The mechanism of exploitation defines the social structure in each period. Moreover, it is obvious that a materialistic theory can never consider the exploiters as mere parasites; in every society divided up into classes, the exploiting of other people's labour constitutes a social function, rendered possible and necessary by the productive mechanism in that society. And a classless society will only be possible if a form of production is achieved which excludes such a function. Besides, no society is ever divided merely into exploiters and exploited, but into several classes, each of which is defined by its relationship to the fundamental fact of exploitation.

Three principal forms of society based on exploitation are known in history: the slave system, the feudal system and the capitalist system. We find only one form of society without exploiters, namely primitive communism, associated with a thoroughly backward technique. The vital question for us is whether, at a higher level, with a highly developed technique, production without exploitation is once again possible. In order to formulate the question correctly, one must know how to study scientifically, not only the various social structures, but above all the transformations which replace one structure by another.

III

What is nowadays called, by a term which seems to invite a good deal of explanation, the class struggle is, of all the conflicts that set human groups at variance, the one with the most serious objective before it. And yet here also purely imaginary entities sometimes intrude themselves which make all guided action impossible, bring nearly all efforts to nought, and almost by themselves alone create the danger of undying hatreds, useless destructions and perhaps unlimited massacres. The struggle of those who obey against those who command, when the mode of commanding entails destroying the human dignity of those underneath, is the most legitimate, most motivated, most genuine action that exists. There has always been this struggle, because those who command always tend, whether they realize it or not, to trample underfoot the human dignity of those below them; the function of commanding, in so far as it is exercised, cannot, save in exceptional circumstances, respect human qualities in the person of executive agents. If its exercise arouses no opposition, it inevitably comes to be exercised as if men were things, albeit exceptionally flexible and manageable things; for when man is under menace of death, which is in the last resort the supreme sanction of all authority, he can become far easier to handle than inanimate matter.

As long as there is a social hierarchy, be that hierarchy what it may, those below will have to struggle, and will struggle, in order not to lose all the rights of a human being. On the other hand, the resistance of those on top to the forces surging up from below, although it naturally invites less sympathy, is founded, at any rate, on concrete motives. In the first place, except in the case of a quite unusual generosity, the privileged necessarily prefer to keep their material and moral privileges intact. And, more especially, those invested with the functions of command have a mission to preserve that order which is indispensable to any social life, and the only possible order in their eyes is the established order. Up to a certain point they are right, for until a new order is in fact set up, no one can affirm that it will be possible; that is precisely why any social progress—great or small—is only possible if the pressure from below is strong enough actually to impose new conditions on social relationships. Thus, between the pressure from below and the resistance from above an unstable balance is continually being established, and it is this which defines at each moment the structure of a given society. However, the encounter of these two opposing forces does not constitute a war, even if here and there a little bloodshed occurs. It is bound to be marked by anger, but not hatred. It may develop into a process of extermination on one side or the other, or on both sides; but then this means that it has changed its nature, and that men's minds have lost sight of the real objects of the struggle, whether because their minds are paralysed by a blind desire for vengeance, or because the intrusion of entities devoid of meaning gives the illusion—always a mistaken one—that a balance is impossible. There is then a catastrophe; but such catastrophes are avoidable. Antiquity has not only bequeathed us the story of the interminable and pointless massacres around Troy, but also the story of the energetic and pacific action by which the Roman plebeians, without spilling a drop of blood, emerged from a condition bordering on slavery and obtained, as the guarantee of their newly-won rights, the institution of the tribunate. It was in precisely the same way that the French workers, by their pacific occupation of the factories,[1] imposed paid holidays, guaranteed wages and workers' delegates.

It is impossible to enumerate all the empty abstractions which today falsify the social struggle, certain of which are in danger of causing it to degenerate into a civil war fatal to both camps. There are too many of them. We can take only one example. Thus, what is going on in the minds of those for whom the word "capitalism" represents absolute evil? We are living under a system that carries with it sometimes crushing forms of coercion and oppression; very painful inequalities; hosts of useless sufferings. On the other hand, this system is economically characterized by a certain relationship between the production and circulation of goods and between the circulation of goods and money.

[1] June 1936.

To what precise extent do these two relationships condition the sufferings in question? To what extent are these due to other causes? To what extent would they be alleviated or aggravated by the setting up of this or that other system? If the problem were to be approached on this basis, we might be able perhaps to discern approximately to what extent capitalism is an evil. As we remain in ignorance on these points, we ascribe all the sufferings we have to undergo or that we observe around us to a few economic phenomena, which are, moreover, continually changing, and which we crystallize arbitrarily in an abstraction impossible to define. In the same way, a worker arbitrarily ascribes all the sufferings he undergoes in the factory to his boss, without asking himself whether under any other system of property the management would not still saddle him with a part of his sufferings or even aggravate some of them; in his case, the struggle "agin the boss" gets mixed up with the irrepressible protest of the human being weighed down by too difficult living conditions. In the other camp, an identical ignorance is responsible for causing all who contemplate the ending of capitalism to be looked upon as agitators, because it is not known to what extent and on what condition the economic relationships that at present constitute capitalism can rightly be considered as necessary to order. Thus the struggle between the opponents and defenders of capitalism is one between blind men; the efforts of the antagonists, on either side, are simply clasping empty space; which is why this struggle is in danger of becoming merciless.

The hunting down of imaginary entities in all spheres of political and social life thus appears as a task necessary in the interests of public health. The effort of clarification with the object of deflating the causes of imaginary conflicts bears no resemblance to the activities of those who use hypnotic charm in an effort to stifle genuine conflicts. It is in fact the exact opposite. The smooth talkers who, while preaching international peace, understand by that expression the indefinite maintenance of the *status quo* to the exclusive advantage of the French State; those who, while recommending social peace, are determined to preserve privileges intact, or at any rate to make any modification dependent on the goodwill of those who enjoy such privileges—such people are the worst enemies of international and civil peace. To discriminate between imaginary antagonisms and genuine antagonisms, to cast discredit on empty abstractions and analyse concrete problems—that, if our contemporaries were to consent to such an intellectual effort, would be to diminish the risks of war without forgoing struggle which, according to Heraclitus, is the condition of life.

IV

Marxism is the highest spiritual expression of bourgeois society. Through it this society attained to a consciousness of itself, in it to a negation of itself. But this negation in its turn could only be expressed in a form determined by the existing order, in a bourgeois form of thought. So it is that each formula of Marxist doctrine lays bare the characteristics of bourgeois society, but at the same time justifies them. By dint of developing a criticism of the capitalist system of economy, Marxism ended by providing the laws of this same economic system with broad foundations; opposition to bourgeois politics ended by claiming for itself the possibility of achieving the old ideal of the bourgeoisie—that ideal which it has realized only in an ambiguous, formal and purely legalistic manner—but of achieving it by fighting against the bourgeoisie, in a truly concrete and more consistent way than the latter; the doctrine which in the beginning was to have served to destroy all ideologies by laying bare the interests which they concealed became itself transformed into an ideology, which was later to be misused for the purpose of deifying the interests of a certain class of bourgeois society.

Thus the same phenomenon has been repeated as at the time when the youthful bourgeoisie began its struggle against feudal and ecclesiastical society. To begin with, it had to cloak its opposition in the religious accoutrements of that same society, and, in order to combat the Church, to claim kinship with primitive Christianity. In the course of its struggle against the two other orders, the bourgeoisie came to recognize the fact that it formed a distinct order, and thereby showed that, despite its opposition to the feudal system, it was conscious of forming an integral part of it (exactly in the same way as the class-consciousness of the modern proletariat, which has arisen to compensate for an unsatisfied propensity to own property, is simply the manifestation of the bourgeois spirit animating proletarians; for the fact of thinking in terms of classes is precisely characteristic of bourgeois society).

The bourgeoisie was only able to free itself of this religious, ecclesiastical and feudal ideology in proportion as feudal society fell into decadence. But it only purified the representation of God of the dross that had accumulated around it since the time when there had been a natural economy; it fashioned for itself a sublimated God who was no longer anything but a transcendent Reason, preceding all events and determining the direction they were to take. In Hegel's philosophy, God still appears, under the name of "world spirit", as mover of history and lawgiver of nature. It was not until after accomplishing its revolution that the bourgeoisie recognized in this God a creation of man himself, and that history is man's own work.

It was Ludwig Feuerbach who clearly formulated this idea; but he was incapable of explaining how it is that "man" comes to make history. For only a mixture of actions can proceed from a juxtaposing of men considered simply as natural beings, but not a regular and ascending development of humanity. Marx's primary and decisive discovery consisted simply in that he went beyond Feuerbach's abstract man and began seeking for the explanation of the historical process in co-operation between individuals, in union and struggle, in the manifold "relationships" that exist between them. However, this progress in thought is still being paid for now, from another point of view, by an unconscious regression. Karl Marx only managed to rise above Feuerbach's isolated "human being" by re-introducing into history, under the name of "society", the God whom Feuerbach had eliminated from it.

Indeed, Marx begins by presenting the new divinity to us in harmless form, as the "totality of social relationships", that is to say as the union of all individual relationships between concrete and active men. He emphasizes on more than one occasion that these "relationships" are, of course, empirical products of human activity, that their "totality", if one absolutely insists on giving a special name to the changing relations which act as a bond of union between active men, must be regarded simply as an abbreviated term designating the result of the historical process. But the deeper Marx's analysis penetrates into the course of history and economic laws, the more his point of view is men's action and thought and is "realized" in their activity. It constitutes, by the side of the "private" sphere of bourgeois individualism, a separate sphere, that of the "general", and, in its capacity as an independent substance, forms the basis of the first; for example, the value of a product is already determined by it, before becoming "realized" in the actual, empirical market price. And under a socialist system, too, there will still be a certain separation between the two spheres. One has only to consider the formula: "individual property on the basis of a collective possession of the land and of the means of production", the formula which defines the future economic order in a well-known passage of *Capital*. The distinction between a general and an individual sphere is here expressly formulated; but it is only possible to visualize a "collective possession" if one regards the collectivity as a particular substance, soaring above individuals and acting through them.

If all this is disputed, one has but to examine closely the Marxist formula: social existence determines consciousness. There are more contradictions in it than words. Seeing that what is "social" can have an existence only in human minds, "social existence" is itself already consciousness; it cannot in addition determine a consciousness which would in any case remain to be defined. To posit in this way a "social existence" as a special determining factor, divorced from our consciousness, hidden no-one knows where, is to make a hypostasis of it; and it constitutes, furthermore, a beautiful example of Marx's tendency towards dualism. But if one wants to consider this enigmatic "existence" as an element of the relationships *between* men, which depends on certain institutions, such as money, one will clearly perceive at once that this element operates only as a *result* of conscious acts performed by individuals, and consequently, far from determining consciousness, is dependent on it. Moreover, if Marx, as opposed to all the thinkers who preceded him, considers it necessary to set on one side a particular form of existence, which he calls "social", it means that he tacitly places it in opposition to the rest of existence, that is to say nature.

CRITICAL EXAMINATION OF THE IDEAS OF REVOLUTION AND PROGRESS[1]

One magic word today seems capable of compensating for all sufferings, resolving all anxieties, avenging the past, curing present ills, summing up all future possibilities: that word is "revolution". It was not coined yesterday. It goes back more than a century and a half. A first attempt to apply it, from 1789 to 1793, produced something, but not what was expected of it. Since then, each generation of revolutionaries has, in its youth, believed itself to be destined to bring about the real revolution, has then gradually grown old and finally died transferring its hopes to succeeding generations; it runs no risk of being proved wrong, since it is dead. This word has aroused such pure acts of devotion, has repeatedly caused such generous blood to be shed, has constituted for so many unfortunates the only source of courage for living, that it is almost a sacrilege to investigate it; all this, however, does not prevent it from possibly being meaningless. It is only for priests that martyrs can be a substitute for proofs.

If one considers the system whose abolition is being called for, it seems that the word "revolution" has never had such an up-to-date significance, for it is obvious that this system is very sick indeed. If one turns towards its possible successors, one finds a paradoxical situation. At the present time there is no organized movement which actually takes the word "revolution" for a watchword determining the direction to be followed by action and propaganda. Yet never before has this watchword been adopted by so many people; and it has a special individual appeal for all who suffer in body or soul from the present conditions of existence, for all who are victims or who simply regard themselves as such, for all, too, who generously take to heart the fate of the victims surrounding them, and for many others besides. This word contains the solution of all the insoluble problems. The havoc caused by the last war, the preparations for a possible future war, weigh with ever greater force upon the peoples of the world; every disturbance in the circulation of money and goods, in credit, in capital investments, results in appalling misery; technical progress seems to bring the mass

[1] This text forms, perhaps, a new version of the beginning of *Reflections on the Causes of Liberty and Social Oppression*. (ED.)

of people more overwork and insecurity than welfare; all this will vanish the moment the hour strikes for the revolution.

The worker who, when in the factory, "finds the hours drag", bound as he is to passive obedience and a dreary and monotonous task, or thinks himself not intended for manual work, or is harried by a superior; or who, outside the factory gates, resents his inability to stand himself such and such a treat available to customers well supplied with money—his thoughts run on the revolution. The unfortunate small shopkeeper, the ruined *rentier*, turn their eyes towards the revolution. The bourgeois adolescent in rebellion against home surroundings and school routine, the intellectual yearning for adventure and suffering from boredom, dream of the revolution. The engineer, whose reason and *amour propre* are alike offended by the priority given to financial over technological considerations, and who wants to see technology ruling the world, longs for the revolution. The majority of those who seriously take to heart liberty, equality and the general welfare, who suffer at the sight of miseries and injustices, await the arrival of a revolution. If one were to take one by one all those who have ever uttered hopefully the word "revolution", to seek out the true motives that have turned each of them in this direction, the precise changes, of a general or personal kind, which they genuinely look forward to, one would discover what an extraordinary variety of ideas and feelings can be covered by the same word. One would see how one man's revolution is not always that of his neighbour—far from it; how the two sorts of revolution are even very often incompatible. One would also find that there is often no connection between the aspirations of all kinds that this word represents in the minds of the men who utter it and the realities to which it is likely to correspond if the future should actually have a social upheaval in store.

At bottom, one thinks nowadays of the revolution, not as a solution to the problems raised at the present time, but as a miracle dispensing one from solving problems. The proof that it is so regarded is that it is expected to drop from the skies; one waits for it to happen, one does not ask oneself who is to bring it about. Few people are simple-minded enough to count in this respect on the big organizations, whether trade union or political, which with more or less conviction continue to claim to represent it. Although their headquarters are not absolutely devoid of capable men, the most optimistic glance cast around them would fail to detect the embryo of a team capable of carrying through a task of these dimensions. Those who form the second rank—the young—show no sign of containing the members of such a team. Anyway, these organizations reflect to a large extent the faults that they denounce in the society in which they are evolving; they even contain other more serious faults, as a result of the influence exerted on them from a distance by a certain totalitarian system worse than the capitalist system. As for the small groups, of extremist or moderate tendency, who accuse the big organizations of doing nothing and display such a touching perseverance in announcing the glad tidings, they would be harder put to it still to designate men capable of presiding at the birth of a new order.

One places one's trust, it is true—or at least one pretends to do so— in the spontaneity of the masses. June 1936 provided a moving example of this spontaneity which one imagined had been wiped out, in France, in the blood of the Commune. A tremendous, ungovernable outburst, springing from the very bowels of the masses, suddenly loosened the vice of social constraint, made the atmosphere at last breathable, changed opinions in all minds, and caused things that six months earlier had been looked upon as scandalous to be accepted as self-evident. Thanks to the incomparable power of persuasion possessed by force, millions of men made it clear—and in the first place to themselves—that they had a share in the sacred rights of humanity, something that even discerning minds had not been able to perceive at the time when they were weak. But that is all. Indeed unless it were to lead towards a more profound upheaval, that is all there could be. The masses do not pose problems, do not solve any; thus they neither organize nor construct. In any case they, too, are profoundly impregnated with the faults of the system under which they live, labour and suffer. Their aspirations bear the imprint of that system. Capitalist society reduces everything to pounds, shillings and pence; the aspirations of the masses are also expressed chiefly in pounds, shillings and pence. The system is based on inequality; the masses give expression to unequal demands. The system is based on coercion; the masses, as soon as they have the right to speak, exercise in their own ranks a similar sort of coercion. It is difficult to see how there could spring up from the masses, spontaneously, the opposite of the system which has formed, or rather deformed, them.

One forms a strange idea in one's mind of the revolution, when one comes to look closely at the matter. Indeed, to say that one forms an idea of it is to say too much. What are the signs by which the revolutionaries think they will be able to recognize the moment when the revolution is actually there? By the barricades and the firing in the streets? By a certain team of men being installed in the government? By the breach of legal forms? By specific acts of nationalization? By the massive exodus of the bourgeoisie? By the issuing of a decree abolishing private property? All that is not clear. However, the fact remains that one awaits, under the name of "revolution", a time when the last shall be first, when the values negated or suppressed by the present system will occupy the forefront, when the slaves, albeit without abandoning their tasks, will be the only citizens, when the social callings at present doomed to submission, obedience and silence will be the first to have the right to say their say and take their part in all matters of public interest. This has nothing to do with religious prophecies. Such a future is represented as corresponding to the normal development of history. This shows that one does not form any correct idea of the normal development of history. Even when one has studied it, one remains filled with vague memories of primary school textbooks and chronological tables.

People cite the example of 1789. We are told that what the bourgeoisie did with regard to the nobility in 1789, the proletariat will do with regard to the bourgeoisie in a year unspecified. People think that in that year 1789, or at any rate between 1789 and 1793, a hitherto subordinate social stratum, the bourgeoisie, drove out and replaced those who ruled society, the kings and nobles. In the same way they think that at a certain moment, designated by the term great invasions, the barbarians invaded the Roman Empire, broke up the Empire's administrative cadres, reduced the Romans to a very inferior status, and took over command everywhere. Why should the proletarians not do the same thing, in their own way? In effect, that is the way things happen in the textbooks. In the textbooks, the Roman Empire lasts up to the beginning of the great invasions; after that, a new chapter opens. In the textbooks, the king, the nobility and the clergy own France until the day when the Bastille falls; after that, it is the Third Estate. For years we have all absorbed this catastrophic notion of history, where the catastrophes are marked by the ends or the beginnings of chapters; we do not get rid of it, and we regulate our action upon it. The division of history textbooks into chapters will cost us many disastrous mistakes.

This division does not correspond to anything of what is known concerning the past. There was no violent substitution of the initial patterns of feudalism for the Roman Empire. In the Empire itself, the barbarians had begun to fill the most important posts, the Romans being gradually reduced to honorary or subordinate positions, the army was disintegrating into armed bands led by adventurers, the system of military colonies was gradually replacing slavery—all this long before the great invasions. Similarly, in 1789, the nobility had already long been reduced to the position of near-parasites. A century earlier, Louis XIV, so haughty in his demeanour towards the highest in the land, would assume a deferential attitude in the presence of a banker. The bourgeoisie occupied the highest positions in the State, reigned in the king's name, filled the magistracy, managed the industrial and commercial undertakings, won renown in the sciences and in literature, and left the nobles with little more than one monopoly, that of the higher appointments in the army. Other examples could be cited.

When it seems that a sanguinary struggle replaces one system by another, this struggle is in reality the crowning point of a transformation that is already more than half accomplished, and brings to power a category of men who already more than half possessed that power. This is a necessity. How could there be a break in the continuity of social life, seeing that we have to eat, clothe ourselves, produce and exchange, command and obey every day, and that all this can only be done today in ways closely similar to those of yesterday? It is under an apparently stable system that changes slowly take place in the structure of social relationships and in the functions allotted to the various social categories. When violent conflicts break out—and they do not always do so—they only play the role of a pair of scales; they hand over power to those who possess it already. Thus it was, to confine ourselves to these two examples, that the great invasions delivered the Roman Empire into the hands of the barbarians, who had already taken possession of it from within, and that the fall of the Bastille, with what followed in its wake, consolidated the modern State—which the kings had set up—by handing the country over to the bourgeoisie, who already did practically everything in it. If the October Revolution, in Russia, seems to have created something altogether new, this is only so in appearance; all it did was to reinforce those powers which were already the only real ones under the Tsars—the bureaucracy, the police, the army. This type of event abolishes those privileges that do not correspond to any effective function, but does not upset the distribution of the functions themselves and of the powers attaching to them. In these days, it might well happen that the financiers, speculators, shareholders, collectors of directorships, small tradesmen, *rentiers*—all these parasites large and small—were one fine day swept away. This might also be accompanied by acts of violence. But how can one believe that those who labour as serfs in the factories and in the mines will promptly change into citizens under a new economic system? It is others, not they, who will reap the benefit of the operation.

Those who claim to base their belief in a revolution on arguments—and even scientific ones—all quote Marx as an authority. The so-called scientific socialism created by Marx has reached the position of a dogma, as indeed have all the results established by modern science, and the conclusions are accepted once and for all, without ever any enquiry into the methods and demonstrations involved. People would rather believe that Marx has demonstrated the future, and imminent, constitution of a socialist society than study his works to see if they can discover there even the remotest attempt at demonstration. True, Marx analyses and takes to pieces with admirable clarity the mechanism of capitalist oppression; but he accounts for it so thoroughly that one can scarcely visualize how, with the selfsame cogs, the mechanism could one fine day transform itself to the point where oppression should progressively begin to disappear.

MEDITATION ON OBEDIENCE AND LIBERTY

The submission of the greater number to the smaller—that fundamental characteristic of nearly every form of social organization—still continues to astonish all who reflect a little. In nature, we see how what is heavier triumphs over what is lighter, how the more prolific species overwhelm the rest. In the case of men, these so clearly marked relations seem to be reversed. Certainly, we know from daily experience that man is not just a fragment of nature, that every day there are kinds of miracles being produced by what is highest in man—will, intelligence and faith. But that is not what we are dealing with here. There is nothing spiritual about that pitiless necessity which has kept, and goes on keeping, the masses of slaves, the masses of poverty-stricken creatures, the masses of underlings on their knees; it corresponds to everything that is brutal in nature. And yet it is apparently exercised in virtue of laws which are contrary to those of nature; as if, in the social balance, the gramme were heavier than the kilogramme.

Nearly four centuries ago, the question was posed by the youthful La Boétie, in his *Contra-un*. He did not answer it. With what moving illustrations could we not support his little book, we who see at the present time, in a country covering a sixth of the globe, a single man bleeding an entire generation! It is when death stalks abroad that the miracle of obedience strikes one so forcibly. That a number of men should submit themselves to a single man through fear of being killed by him is astonishing enough; but what are we to make of it when they remain submissive to him to the point of dying at his orders? When there are at least as many risks attached to obedience as there are to rebellion, how is obedience maintained?

Knowledge of the material world in which we live was able to develop from the moment when Florence, after producing so many other marvels, brought mankind, through Galileo, the notion of force. It was then also only that the equipping of the material side of life by industry could be undertaken. And we, who claim to set about equipping the social side of life, will not have even the crudest knowledge of it as long as we have not formed a clear notion of social force. Society cannot have its engineers as long as it has not first had its Galileo. Is there at the present time, over the whole of the earth's surface, a single mind which can conceive even vaguely how it is that one man in the Kremlin has the power to cause any head whatever to fall within the confines of the Russian frontiers?

Marxists have not helped towards forming a clear view of the problem by picking out economics as the key to the social riddle. If one considers a society as a collective being, then this great beast, like all other beasts, can principally be defined by the way in which it makes sure of its food, sleep, shelter from the elements—in short, its life. But society considered in its relation to the individual cannot be defined simply by the methods of production. However much you may resort to all kinds of subtleties to show that war is an essentially economic phenomenon, it is palpably obvious that war is destruction and not production. Obedience and command are also phenomena for which the conditions of production do not provide a sufficient explanation. When an old working man, unemployed and left to starve, dies quietly in the street or some slum, this submission which extends to the very point of death cannot be explained by the play of vital necessities. The massive destruction of wheat and of coffee during the crisis furnishes a no less clear example. The notion of force and not that of need is the key to an understanding of social phenomena.

Galileo had no cause to congratulate himself, as far as he personally was concerned, for having put so much genius and so much integrity into deciphering nature; but at any rate he only found himself up against a handful of powerful men specialized in the interpretation of the Scriptures. The study of the social mechanism, on the other hand, is hampered by passions that are found in all and each of us. There is hardly anyone who does not desire either to overthrow or to preserve the present relations between the functions of command and submission. Both of these desires befog the mind's scrutiny and prevent one from perceiving the lessons of history, which everywhere shows us the masses under the yoke and a few raising the lash.

Some—those on the side which addresses its appeal to the masses—wish to show that such a situation is not only iniquitous, but also impossible, at any rate in the near or distant future. Others—on the side which wants to preserve order and established privileges—wish to show that the yoke is light, or even that it is consented to. On both sides, a veil is thrown over the fundamental absurdity of the social mechanism, instead of looking this apparent absurdity fairly in the face and analysing it so as to discover in it the secret of the machine. Whatever may be the subject under investigation, there is no other method for thinking about it. Wonder is the father of wisdom, Plato said.

Since the many obey, and obey to the point of allowing suffering and death to be inflicted on them, while the few command, this means that it is not true that number constitutes a force. Number, whatever our imagination may lead us to believe, is a weakness. Weakness is on the side where people are hungry, exhausted, where they implore and tremble, not on the side where they live comfortably, bestow favours, and issue threats. The masses are not in subjection despite the fact of their being number, but because they are number. If there is a street fight between one man against twenty, the man will probably be left on the ground for dead. But at a sign from a white man, twenty Annamite coolies can be flogged, one after the other, by one or two foremen,

The contradiction is perhaps only apparent. No doubt on all occasions those who command are fewer than those who obey. But precisely because they are few they form a whole. The others, precisely because they are too many, are one plus one plus one, and so on. Thus the power of an infinitesimal minority is based, in spite of everything, on the force of number. This minority is far stronger in number than each one of those who go to form the herd of the majority. It must not be concluded from this that organization of the masses would reverse the relation; for such is impossible. It is only possible to establish cohesion between a limited number of men. Beyond that, there is no longer anything but a juxtaposing of individuals—that is to say weakness.

There are, however, certain moments when it is not so. At certain moments in history, a great rush of wind sweeps over the masses; their breath, their words, their movements are merged together. Then nothing is able to resist them. The mighty know in their turn, at last, what it is to feel alone and defenceless; and they tremble. Tacitus, in a few immortal pages describing a military mutiny, analysed the matter perfectly. "The principal sign that it was a deep-seated movement, impossible to quell, was that they were not scattered about or controlled by a few individuals, but flared up as one man, fell silent as one man, with such unanimity and constancy that one would have thought they were acting upon a word of command." We all witnessed a miracle of this kind in June 1936, and the impression it made has not yet been effaced.

Such moments do not last, although the downtrodden ardently hope to see them last for ever. They cannot last, because that unanimity which is produced in the heat of a quickening and general emotion is incompatible with any form of methodical action. Its effect is always to suspend all action and arrest the daily course of life. This temporary stoppage cannot be prolonged; the course of daily life has to be taken up again, the daily tasks have to be performed. The mass dissolves once more into individuals, the memory of its victory fades, the erstwhile situation, or its equivalent, is gradually re-established; and although it may be that in the interval there has been a change of masters, it is always the same ones who have to obey.

The powerful have no interest more vital than to prevent this crystallization of the subject masses, or at any rate, for they cannot always prevent it, to make it as rare as possible. It often happens in the natural course of things that a great many of the downtrodden are swept by the same emotion at the same time; but as a rule this emotion has barely had the time to awaken when it is repressed by the feeling of an irremediable impotence. The first article of skilful policy on the part of the masters is to foster this feeling of impotence.

The human mind is incredibly flexible, prompt to imitate, to bow to outside circumstances. The man who obeys, whose movements, pains, pleasures are determined by the word of another, feels himself to be inferior, not by accident, but by nature. At the other end of the scale there is a like feeling of superiority, and these twin illusions reinforce each other. It is impossible for the most heroically staunch mind to preserve the consciousness of an inward value when there is no external fact on which this consciousness can be based. Christ himself, when he found himself abandoned by everybody, mocked, despised, his life counted for naught, lost for a moment the feeling of his mission. What other meaning can be attached to the cry: "My God, my God, why hast thou forsaken me?" It seems to those who obey that some mysterious inferiority has predestined them to obey from all eternity, and every mark of scorn—even the tiniest—which they suffer at the hands of their superiors or their equals, every order they receive, and especially every act of submission they themselves perform confirms them in this feeling.

Everything that contributes towards giving those who are at the bottom of the social scale the feeling that they possess a value is to a certain extent subversive. The myth of Soviet Russia is subversive in so far as it can give the communist factory worker who is sacked by his foreman the feeling that, in spite of all, he has behind him the Red Army and Magnitogorsk, and thus enable him to preserve his pride. The myth of the historically inevitable revolution plays the same, though a more abstract, role; it is something, when one is lonely and miserable, to have history on one's side. Christianity, too, when it first began, was dangerous to the established order. It did not inspire the poor, the slaves, with the desire for power and the goods of this world—quite the opposite; but it gave them the feeling of an inner value which put them on the same level as or higher than the rich, and that was enough to place the social hierarchy in danger. It very quickly mended its ways, learnt how to make the proper distinction between the marriage and burial ceremonies for the rich and those for the poor, and to relegate the unfortunate to the back seats.

Social force is bound to be accompanied by lies. That is why all that is highest in human life, every effort of thought, every effort of love, has a corrosive action on the established order. Thought can just as readily, and on as good grounds, be stigmatized as revolutionary on the one side, as counter-revolutionary on the other. In so far as it is ceaselessly creating a scale of values "that is not of this world", it is the enemy of the forces which control society. But it is no more favourably disposed towards undertakings which tend to disrupt or transform society, and which, before ever they have succeeded, must necessarily imply for those who pursue them the subjection of the many to the few, the disdain of the privileged for the anonymous masses, and the handling of lies. Genius, love, holiness, fully deserve the reproach that is often levelled at them of tending to destroy what is without building up anything in its place. As for those who want to think, love, and transpose in all purity into political action what their mind and heart inspire them with, they can only perish murdered, forsaken even by their own people, vilified after their death by history, as happened to the Gracchi.

Such a state of things results in profound and irremediable spiritual torture for every man with the public welfare at heart. Participation, even from a distance, in the play of forces which control the movement of history is not possible without contaminating oneself or incurring certain defeat. Nor is it possible, without great lack of conscientiousness, to take refuge in indifference or in an ivory tower. Thus there remains the formula of the "lesser evil", so discredited by the use which the social-democrats have made of it, as the only one applicable, provided it be applied with the coldest lucidity.

The social order, though necessary, is essentially evil, whatever it may be. You cannot reproach those whom it crushes for undermining it as much as they can; when they resign themselves to it, it is not through strength of character but, on the contrary, as the result of a humiliation which extinguishes the virile qualities in them. Neither can you reproach those who organize it for defending it, or make them out to be forming a conspiracy against the general welfare. The struggles between fellow citizens do not spring from a lack of understanding or goodwill; they belong to the nature of things, and cannot be appeased, but can only be smothered by coercion. For anyone who loves liberty, it is not desirable that they should disappear, but only that they should remain short of a certain limit of violence.

ON THE CONTRADICTIONS OF MARXISM

To my mind, it is not events which make a revision of Marxism a necessity, it is Marx's doctrine, which, because of the gaps and inconsistencies it contains, is and has always been far inferior to the role people have wanted to make it play; which does not mean to say that either then or since anything better has been worked out. It is the recollection of my own personal experience that leads me to express so categorical a judgment, and one so calculated to cause offence. When, in my youth, I read *Capital* for the first time, I was immediately struck by certain gaps, certain contradictions of the first importance. Their very obviousness, at that time, prevented me from placing confidence in my own judgment; I said to myself that so many great minds that have embraced Marxism must also have perceived these patently clear gaps and inconsistencies; that therefore the former must certainly have been filled in, the latter resolved, in other works on Marxist doctrine. How many young minds are not thus led, through lack of self-confidence, to stifle their most justified doubts? As for me, in the years that followed, the study of Marxist literature, of Marxist parties or those which go by that name, and of events themselves, was only able to confirm me in the judgment formed in my youth. So it is not by comparison with the facts, but in itself, that I consider Marxist doctrine to be defective; or rather, I think that the body of writings by Marx, Engels and those who have taken them as guides does not constitute a doctrine.

There is a contradiction, an obvious, glaring contradiction, between Marx's analytic method and his conclusions. This is not surprising; he worked out the conclusions before the method. Hence Marxism's claim to be a science is rather amusing. Marx became a revolutionary in his youth, under the influence of noble sentiments; his ideal at this period was, indeed, humane, clear, conscious, reasoned, quite as much as—and even considerably more than—during the subsequent years of his life. Later, he tried to work out a method for studying human societies. His vigorous mind did not allow him to manufacture a mere caricature of a method; he saw, or at any rate glimpsed, an authentic method. Such are the two contributions he made to the history of thought: in his youth, he perceived a new formula for the social ideal, and in his maturity, the new or partly new formula of a method for interpreting history. He thus gave double proof of genius. Unfortunately, loth, as all strong characters are, to allow two separate men to go on living in him—the revolutionary and the scientist; averse also to that sort of hypocrisy which adherence to an ideal unaccompanied by action implies; insufficiently scrupulous, moreover, in regard to his own thought, he insisted on making his method into an instrument for predicting a future in conformity with his desires. To achieve this, he was obliged to give a twist both to the method and to the ideal, to deform the one and the other. In the slackening of his thought which permitted such deformations, he allowed himself—he, the nonconformist—to be carried away into an unconscious conformity with the most ill-founded superstitions of his day, the cult of production, the cult of big industry, the blind belief in progress. He thus dealt a serious and lasting, maybe irreparable blow—at any rate one difficult to repair—both to the scientific and to the revolutionary spirit. I do not think that the workers' movement in this country will become something living again until it seeks, I will not say doctrines, but a source of inspiration, in what Marx and Marxists have fought against and very foolishly despised: in Proudhon, in the workers' groups of 1848, in the trade-union tradition, in the anarchist spirit. As for a doctrine, the future alone, at best, will perhaps be able to provide one; not the past.

Marx's ideas about revolutions can be expressed thus: a revolution takes place at the moment when it is already nearly accomplished; it is when the structure of a society has ceased to correspond to its institutions that these change and are replaced by others which reflect the new structure. In particular, the section of society which the revolution places in power is the same as that which already, before the revolution, although victimized by the prevailing institutions, in fact played the most active role. Broadly speaking, "historical materialism", so often misunderstood, means that institutions are determined by the actual mechanism of the relations between men, which in turn depends on the form taken at each moment by the relations between man and nature, that is to say on the way in which production is carried out; production of consumer goods, production of the means of production, and also—an important point, although Marx leaves it undeveloped—production of the means of making war. Men are not the impotent playthings of fate; they are eminently active beings; but their activity is at each moment limited by the structure of the society which they form among themselves, and only modifies that structure in its turn by a ricochet, once it has modified the relations between them and nature. The social structure can never be modified except indirectly.

On the other hand, the analysis of the present system—an analysis that is found scattered through several of Marx's works—fixes the source of the cruel oppression suffered by the workers not in men, nor in institutions, but in the very mechanism of social relations. If the workers are exhausted by fatigue and want, this is because they do not count for anything and the growth of the factories counts for everything. They do not count for anything because the role that the majority of them play in production is that of mere cogs, and they are degraded to this role of cogs because intellectual labour has become separated from manual labour, and because the development of machinery has taken away the privilege of skill from man so as to transfer it to inert matter. The growth of the factory counts for everything, because the spur of competition is continually forcing factories to expand in order to subsist; consequently "the relationship between consumption and production is reversed", "consumption is only a necessary evil"; and if the workers are not paid according to the value of their labour, this is simply the result of the "reversal of the relationship between subject and object" which sacrifices man to lifeless machinery and makes production of the means of production the supreme aim.

The role of the State leads to a similar analysis. If the State is oppressive, if democracy is a delusion, it is because the State is composed of three permanent bodies, recruited by co-option and distinct from the people, namely, the army, the police and the bureaucracy. The interests of these three bodies are different from those of the population and consequently opposed to them. It follows that the "State machine" is oppressive by its very nature, its mechanism cannot function without crushing the citizens; the best will in the world cannot turn it into an instrument for the public good; the only way to stop it from being oppressive is to smash it. Moreover—and in this matter Marx's analysis is less rigorous—the oppression exercised by the State machine is identical with that exercised by big industry; this machine is automatically at the service of the principal social force, namely, capital, or in other words the equipment of industrial undertakings. Those who are sacrificed to the development of industrial equipment, that is to say the proletariat, are also those who are exposed to the full brutality of the State, and the State keeps them by force in the position of slaves of the undertakings.

What are we to conclude? The conclusion forces itself on the mind: nothing of all this can be abolished by means of a revolution; on the contrary, all this must have disappeared before a revolution can take place; or if it does take place beforehand, it will only be an apparent revolution which will leave oppression intact or even increase it. Yet Marx reached precisely the opposite conclusion; he concluded that society was ripe for a revolution of liberation. Do not let us forget that nearly a hundred years ago he already thought such a revolution to be imminent. On this point at any rate he has been strikingly refuted by events, strikingly so in Europe and in America, still more strikingly so in Russia. But the refutation provided by events was scarcely necessary; in Marx's doctrine itself the contradiction was so striking that it is surprising neither he, nor his friends, nor his followers became aware of it. How were the factors of oppression, so closely bound up with the actual mechanism of social life, suddenly to disappear? How, given big industry, machinery and the degradation of manual labour, could the workers be anything but mere cogs in the factories? How, if they continued to be mere cogs, could they at the same time become the "ruling class"? How, given the techniques of war, policing and administration, could the military, police and administrative functions cease to be specialized callings, professions, and consequently the prerogative of "permanent bodies, distinct from the population"? Or else must we assume a transformation of industry, of machinery, of the technique of manual labour, that of administration, that of war? But such transformations are slow, gradual; they are not the result of a revolution.

One can say that to such questions which immediately follow from Marx's analyses, neither Marx, nor Engels, nor their disciples provided the least answer. They passed them over in silence. In regard to one point only did Marx and Engels draw attention to a possible transition from the capitalist system towards a better form of society; they thought they saw that the very development of competition must bring about automatically, and in a brief space, the disappearance of competition and at the same time that of capitalistic property. In effect, the concentration of undertakings was taking place under their eyes, just as it still is under ours. Seeing that it is competition which, under the capitalist system, turns the expansion of undertakings into an end, and men, whether considered as producers or consumers, into a mere means, they could indeed regard the disappearance of competition as equivalent to that of the system itself. But they reasoned wrongly in one respect; just because competition, which causes the small to be devoured by the big, gradually reduces the number of competitors, you cannot therefore conclude that this number must one day necessarily be reduced to one. Moreover, Marx and Engels, in their analysis, omitted one factor: war. Marxists have never analysed the phenomenon of war, nor its relation to the economic system; for I do not call the simple assertion that capitalist greed is the cause of wars an analysis. What a gap! And what credence can be given to a theory which claims to be scientific and is capable of such an omission? For since industrial production is nowadays not only the chief source of wealth but also the chief means of carrying on war, the result is that it is subjected not only to competition between undertakings but to a still more urgent and imperative competition—that between nations. How is that competition to be abolished? Must it, like the other, abolish itself by the progressive elimination of competitors? Must we wait, in order to be able to look forward to socialism, for the day when the world will find itself under the *pax Germanica* or the *pax Japonica*? That day is not near at hand, if it is indeed ever to come, and the parties which claim to represent socialism do everything possible to postpone it.

The problems which Marxism has failed to solve have not been solved by events, either; they have, in fact, become more and more acute. Although the workers live better than they did in Marx's day—at any rate in countries peopled by the white race, for it is a different story, alas, in the colonies; and even Russia must perhaps be excepted—the obstacles in the way of their liberation are more difficult to overcome now than then. The Taylor system and those that have followed it have reduced the workers to a far greater extent than before to the position of mere cogs in the factories, except for a few highly-skilled jobs. Manual labour, in the majority of cases, is still farther removed from the work of a craftsman, still more divested of intelligence and skill; machines are still more oppressive. The arms race calls still more imperiously for the sacrifice of the people as a whole to industrial production. The State machine develops day by day in a more monstrous fashion, becomes day by day farther and farther removed from the mass of the population, blinder, more inhuman. Any country that attempted a socialist revolution would be very quickly compelled, in order to defend itself against the rest, to reproduce in magnified form all the cruelties of the system it had set out to abolish, unless the revolution were to spread. Doubtless such a contagion may be expected, but it would have to occur immediately or not at all; for a revolution that has degenerated into a tyranny ceases to be contagious; and, among other obstacles in the way, the exacerbation of nationalist feeling prevents one from being able reasonably to believe in the immediate extension of a revolution in several big countries.

Thus the contradiction between the method of analysis elaborated by Marx and the revolutionary hopes that he announced seems still sharper today than in his time. What are we to conclude from this?

Must there be a revision of Marxism? One cannot revise something which does not exist, and there has never been such a thing as Marxism, but only a series of incompatible assertions, some of them well founded, others not; unfortunately, the best founded are the least palatable. We are still asked if such a revision should bear a revolutionary stamp. But what do we understand by the word "revolutionary"? It is capable of a good many interpretations. Does being a revolutionary mean expecting in the near future some blessed catastrophe, some upheaval which realizes on this earth a part of the promises contained in the Gospels, and gives us finally a society wherein the last shall be first? If that is what it means, then I am not a revolutionary, for such a future—which incidentally would overwhelm me with joy—is to my mind, if not impossible, at any rate altogether improbable; and I do not think that anyone can nowadays have solid, serious reasons for being a revolutionary in this sense.

Or else does being a revolutionary mean calling forth by one's wishes and helping by one's acts everything which can, directly or indirectly, alleviate or lift the weight that presses upon the mass of men, break the chains that degrade labour, reject the lies by means of which it is sought to disguise or excuse the systematic humiliation of the majority? In that event it is a case of an ideal, a judgment of value, something willed, and not of an interpretation of human history and of the social mechanism. Taken in this sense, the revolutionary spirit is as old as oppression itself and will go on for as long, even longer; for if oppression should disappear, it will have to continue in order to prevent its reappearance; it is eternal; it has no need to undergo a revision, but it can become enriched, sharpened, and it must be purified of all the extraneous accretions that can come to disguise and corrupt it. This eternal spirit of revolt which quickened the Roman plebeians, which fired almost simultaneously, towards the end of the fourteenth century, the wool workers of Florence, the English peasantry, the artisans of Ghent, what can it take and assimilate from the works of Marx? It has to take from thence precisely that which has been almost forgotten by what is called Marxism: the glorification of productive labour, considered as man's highest activity; the assertion that only a society wherein the act of work brought all man's faculties into play, wherein the man who works occupied the front rank, would realize human greatness to the full. We find, in Marx's early writings, lines concerning labour that have a lyrical accent; we also find some in Proudhon and in certain poets, in Goethe, in Verhaeren. This new poetry, appropriate to our time, which forms perhaps its chief claim to greatness, must not be lost. Therein the oppressed must find evoked their own mother-country, which is hope.

But in other respects Marxism has seriously debased that spirit of revolt which, in the last century, shone with so pure a light in our country. It has mingled with it at the same time flashy pseudo-scientific trimmings, a messianic eloquence, an unfettering of appetites that have disfigured it. Nothing entitles one to assure the workers that science is on their side. Science is for them, as indeed for everyone today, that mysterious power which has, in a single century, transformed the face of the world through industrial technique; when they are told that science is on their side, they immediately think they possess an unlimited source of power. Nothing of the kind! You do not find among the communists, socialists or trade-unionists of this or that tendency any clearer or more accurate knowledge of our society and its mechanism than you do among the bourgeois, conservatives or fascists. Even if the workers' organizations were superior in the matter of knowledge, which is not at all the case, they would not for that reason have in their hands the indispensable means of action; science is nothing, in actual fact, without technical resources, and it does not bestow them, it only enables one to make use of them. It would be still more erroneous to maintain that science makes it possible to predict the triumph of the workers' cause in the near future; it is not so, and you cannot even believe in good faith that it is so unless you resolutely shut your eyes. Nothing entitles one either to assure the workers that they have a mission, an "historic task", as Marx used to say; that it is up to them to save the world. There is no reason to attribute to them such a mission, any more than to the slaves of antiquity or the serfs of the Middle Ages. Like the slaves, like the serfs, they are unhappy, unjustly so; it is well that they defend themselves; it would be better if they could liberate themselves; and that is all that can be said about it. These illusions that are showered on them, in a language that mixes together religious and scientific commonplaces in deplorable fashion, are fatal to them. For they lead them to believe that things are going to be easy, that they have a modern god called Progress to push them from behind and a modern providence called History to do the donkey work for them. Finally, nothing entitles one to promise them, at the end of their liberation effort, enjoyments and power. A certain facile irony has done considerable harm by pouring cold water on the lofty idealism, the almost ascetic spirit animating socialist groups at the beginning of the nineteenth century; it has only succeeded in degrading the working class.

FRAGMENTS,[1] LONDON 1943

I

Contradiction in matter is imaged by the clash between opposing forces. That movement towards the good, through contradictions, which Plato described as being that of the thinking creature aided by a supernatural grace, was attributed by Marx purely and simply to matter, but to a certain type of matter—social matter.

He was struck by the fact that social groups manufacture moralities for their own use, thanks to which the specific activity of each one is placed outside the reach of evil. There is thus the morality of the soldier, that of the business man, and so on, whose first article consists in denying that it is possible to commit any evil while waging war, doing business, etc., according to the rules. Furthermore, all the conceptions that are current in any society whatsoever are influenced by the specific morality of the group which dominates that society. That is something which has always been known, and of which Plato, for example, was fully aware.

Once it has been recognized, there are several ways of reacting to it,

---

[1] These are composed of loose pages found among Simone Weil's papers after her death, which we publish as they stand. Certain passages in them figure again in the last essay of the book. (ED.)

according to the depth of one's moral uneasiness. It can be recognized as far as others are concerned, but ignored as far as oneself is concerned. This simply means that one accepts as an absolute value the specific morality of the social group of which one happens to be a member. One's mind is then at rest; but morally speaking one is dead. This happens very frequently. Or else one may realize the miserable weakness of every human mind; one is then seized with anguish. Some, in order to escape from this anguish, are ready to allow the words "good" and "evil" to lose all significance: such people at the end of a longer or shorter time rot away, become putrefied. This is perhaps what would have happened to Montaigne but for the influence of his Stoic friend. Others seek anxiously, desperately, a road by which to escape from the sphere of relative moralities and know the absolute good. Amongst these one can name men of very unequal merit, such as Plato, Pascal and, however strange it may seem, Marx.

The true road exists. Plato and many others have followed it. But it is open only to those who, recognizing themselves to be incapable of finding it, give up looking for it, and yet do not cease to desire it to the exclusion of everything else. To these it is given to feed on a good which, being situated outside this world, is not subject to any social influence whatever. It is the transcendental bread mentioned in the original text of the Lord's Prayer.

Marx went in search of something else, and believed he had found it. Since lies in moral affairs emanate from individual groups each of which seeks to posit its own existence as an absolute good, he told himself that on the day when there were no more individual groups there would be no more lies. He assumed, quite arbitrarily, that the collision between social forces would automatically bring about this destruction of groups. Feeling irresistibly that a knowledge of justice and truth is in some sort man's due, for his craving for them is too deeply seated to admit of a refusal; having rightly recognized that no human mind, without any exception, has sufficient strength to escape from the factors of falsehood which poison social life; unaware that there exists a source whence such strength descends upon those who desire it with complete humility, he assumed that society, by an automatic process of growth, would eliminate its own toxins. He assumed it without any reason save that he could not do otherwise.

It is thus that we must understand what often appears in him as the negation of the very concepts of truth, justice, moral value. Since society is still poisoned, no mind is capable of attaining to truth and justice. Those who utter these words are liars or dupes of liars. He who desires to serve justice has only one method, namely, to hasten forward the operation of the mechanism that will bring about a non-poisoned society. It matters little what means he employs to this end; they are good, provided they are effective. Thus Marx, exactly in the same way as the business men of his time or the warriors of the Middle Ages, arrived at a morality which placed the social category to which he belonged—that of professional revolutionaries—above sin. He fell into the very weakness which he had tried so hard to avoid, as happens to all who seek moral strength where it is not to be found.

As for the nature of this mechanism for producing paradise, he deduced it by an almost puerile form of reasoning. When a dominant group ceases to dominate, it is replaced by another group which previously found itself naturally lower in the scale. As this process is repeated, social development finally brings the very lowest group to the top. Then there is no longer anything below, no more oppression; there are no more group interests opposed to the general interest, no more lies.

In other words, as the result of an evolution in the course of which force has changed hands, one day the weak, having remained such, will have force on their side. Here we have a particularly absurd example of the tendency to extrapolate which was one of the defects of the science and of all the thought of the nineteenth century, when, except among pure mathematicians, the notion of limit was unknown.

When force changes hands, it still remains a relation of stronger to weaker, a relation of dominance. It can go on changing hands indefinitely, without a single term of the relation being eliminated. At the moment when a political transformation occurs, those who make ready to take over power are already in possession of a force, that is to say a dominance over weaker men. If they possess none at all, power will not pass into their hands, unless an effective factor other than force should intervene; which Marx did not admit as possible. In short, Marx's revolutionary materialism consists in positing, on the one hand, that force alone governs social relations to the exclusion of anything else, and, on the other hand, that one day the weak, while remaining the weak, will nevertheless be the stronger. He believed in miracles without believing in the supernatural. From a purely rationalist point of view, if one believes in miracles, it is better to believe in God as well.

What lies at the bottom of Marx's thought is a contradiction. Which does not mean to say that absence of contradiction is a criterion of truth. Quite the opposite; contradiction, as Plato knew, is the sole instrument of developing thought. But there is a legitimate and an illegitimate use of contradiction. The illegitimate use consists in combining incompatible assertions as if they were compatible. The legitimate use consists, when the human intelligence is faced with the necessity of accepting two incompatible truths, in recognizing them as such, and in making of them as it were the two arms of a pair of pincers, an instrument for entering indirectly into contact with the sphere of transcendent truth inaccessible to our intelligence. Contradiction handled in this way plays an essential role in Christian dogma. It would be easy to demonstrate this with regard to the Trinity, to take one example. It plays a similar role in other traditions. Here perhaps is a criterion for discerning which religious or philosophical traditions are authentic.

The essential contradiction in the human condition is that man is subject to force, and craves for justice. He is subject to necessity, and craves for the good. It is not his body alone that is thus subject, but all his thoughts as well; and yet man's very being consists in straining towards the good. That is why we all believe that there is a unity between necessity and the good. Some believe that the thoughts of man concerning the good possess the highest degree of force here below; these are known as idealists. They are doubly mistaken, first in that these thoughts are without force, and secondly in that they do not lay hold of the good. These thoughts are influenced by force; so that this attitude is in the end a less energetic replica of the contrary attitude. Others believe that force is of itself directed towards the good; these are idolaters. This is the belief of all materialists who do not sink into the state of indifference. They are also doubly mistaken; first force is a stranger to and indifferent to the good, and secondly it is not always and everywhere the stronger. They alone can escape these errors who have recourse to the incomprehensible notion that there is a unity between necessity and the good, in other words, between reality and the good, outside this world. These last also believe that something of this unity communicates itself to those who direct towards it their attention and their desire—a notion still more incomprehensible, but verified experimentally.

Marx was an idolater. The object of his idolatry was the society of the future; but, since every idolater needs a present object, he transferred his idolatry to that fraction of society which he believed to be on the verge of bringing about the expected transformation—the proletariat. He considered himself to be its natural leader, at any rate as far as theory and general strategy were concerned; but in another sense he thought he received the light from it. If he had been asked why, seeing that all thinking is subject to the fluctuations of force, he, Marx, like a great number of his contemporaries, was continually thinking of a perfectly just society, he would readily have found the answer. In his view, this was a mechanical result of the transformation that was preparing and which, although not yet accomplished, was in a sufficiently advanced state of germination to be reflected in the thoughts of a few. He interpreted in the same way the thirst for absolute justice so burningly present among the workers of that period.

In a sense he was right. Nearly all the socialists of that time, himself included, would doubtless have been incapable of placing themselves on the side of the weakest if, in addition to the compassion aroused by weakness, there had not been the prestige that accompanies an appearance of force. This prestige came not from a prevision of the future but from a recent past, from a few dazzling and deceptive scenes of the French Revolution.

The facts prove that nearly always men's thoughts are fashioned—as Marx thought—by the lies involved in social morality. Nearly always, but not quite always. That too is certain. Twenty-five centuries ago, certain Greek philosophers, whose very names are unknown to us, affirmed that slavery is absolutely contrary both to reason and to nature. Obvious as are the fluctuations of morality in accordance with time and place, it is equally obvious also that the morality which proceeds directly from mystic thought is one, identical, unchangeable. This can be verified by turning to Egypt, Greece, India, China, Buddhism, the Moslem tradition, Christianity and the folklore of all countries. This morality is unchangeable because it is a reflection of the absolute good that is situated outside this world. It is true that all religions, without exception, have concocted impure mixtures of this morality and social morality, in varying doses. It constitutes nevertheless the experimental proof on earth that the pure transcendental good is real; in other words, the experimental proof of the existence of God.

II

Marx's really outstanding work is the application of his method to the study of the society around him. He defined with admirable precision the relationships of force in that society. He demonstrated that wage-earning is a form of oppression, that the workers are inevitably enslaved under a system of production where, deprived of knowledge and skill, they are reduced practically to nothing before the stupendous combination of science and natural forces which is, as it were, crystallized in the machine. He demonstrated that the State, being made up of categories of men distinct from the population—bureaucracy, police, military cadres—itself forms a machine that automatically crushes those whom it claims to represent. He perceived that economic life was itself going to become more and more centralized and bureaucratic, thus bringing together the leaders of production and those in charge of the State.

These premises ought to have led him to foresee the modern phenomenon of the totalitarian State and the nature of the doctrines that were to spring up around it. But Marx wanted this sombre mechanism to bring about justice, which is why he did not wish to foresee the future. So he accepted the most blatant absurdity, the one most opposed to his own principles. He assumed that, though everything is governed by force, a proletariat lacking force was nevertheless going to carry through a successful political *coup d'état*, follow it up by a purely legal measure, namely, the abolition of individual property, and as a result achieve the mastery in all fields of social life.

Yet he had himself described this proletariat as despoiled of everything except its feeble hands for performing servile tasks and its ardent thirst for justice. He had shown how the forces of nature, canalized by machinery, monopolized by the masters of industrial undertakings, reduce mere muscular strength almost to nothing; how modern culture, by fixing a gulf between manual and intellectual work, condemns the minds of the workers to banishment among objects devoid of value; how manual skill itself had been taken away from men and transferred to the machines. He had shown with pitiless clarity that this technique, this culture, this organization of labour and of social life form the chains that keep the workers enslaved. And at the same time he wanted to believe that, with all this remaining intact, the proletariat would break its servitude and take over command.

This belief is as much opposed to Marx's materialist prejudices as it is to the solid, permanent part of his thought. It follows immediately from his most searching analyses that the transformation of production, intellectual culture and social organization must in general precede the overthrow of political and legal systems, as was the case in the Revolution of 1789. But Marx refused to see this consequence, obvious as it was, because it went contrary to his desires. There was no fear of his disciples seeing it, either, for the same reason.

As for the Marxist interpretation of history, nothing can be said about it, because there is none. No attempt was made to explain the evolution of civilization in terms of the development of the means of production. What is more, while positing that the class struggle is the key to history, Marx did not even attempt to show that this is a materialist principle of explanation. This is by no means self-evident. The human soul's longing for liberty, its craving for power, can equally well be analysed as facts of a spiritual order.

In pasting the label "class struggle" on to these facts, Marx merely simplified things in an almost puerile manner. He left out war, a factor in human history as important as the social struggle. Hence the fact that Marxists have always found themselves ludicrously confused before all the problems posed by war. For that matter, this omission is typical of the whole of the nineteenth century; in committing it, Marx gave yet another proof of intellectual servility to the dominating influences of his age. Similarly, he chose to forget that the conflicts of the oppressed among themselves, of the oppressors among themselves, are as important as the mutual conflicts between oppressed and oppressors, and that in any case, more often than not, the same human being is both at once. He made oppression the central notion of his writings, but never attempted to analyse it. He never asked himself what it is.

What has caused the stupendous political success of Marxism is above all this juxtaposing of two meagre, sketchy and mutually incompatible doctrines. Humanity has always placed in God its hope of quenching its thirst for justice. Once God no longer inhabited men's souls, that hope had either to be discarded or to be placed in matter. Man cannot bear to be alone in willing the good. He needs an all-powerful ally. If this ally is not spirit, it will be matter. It is simply a case of two different expressions of the same fundamental thought. But the second expression is defective. It is a badly constructed religion. But it is a religion. There is, therefore, nothing surprising in the fact that Marxism has always possessed a religious character. It has a great many things in common with the forms of religious life most bitterly attacked by Marx, especially in having frequently been used, to quote Marx's own formula, as the opium of the people. But it is a religion devoid of *mystique*, in the true sense of the word.

Not only materialism in general, but the brand of materialism peculiar to Marx, was bound to guarantee him an immense influence. The nineteenth century believed that in industrial production lay the key to human progress. It was the thesis upheld by the economists, the conception that enabled industrialists, without the least qualm of conscience, to bring about the death through exhaustion of generations of children. Marx simply took over this conception and transferred it to the revolutionary camp, thus preparing for the emergence of a quite singular type of bourgeois revolutionary.

But it was left to our own age to make the maximum use of Marx's works. The idealistic, utopian doctrine contained therein is immensely valuable for stirring up the masses, making them carry a political party to power, keeping youth in that state of permanent enthusiasm necessary to every totalitarian régime. At the same time the other doctrine, the materialist doctrine which freezes all human aspirations under the cold metallic touch of force, provides a totalitarian State with a great number of excellent answers when faced with the timid aspirations of the people. Generally speaking, the mental juxtaposition of an idealism and a materialism, each equally superficial and vulgar, constitutes the spiritual character—if one may be permitted this term—of our time.

The vice of such a conception is not the combination of materialism and idealism, for they have to be combined; it is the placing of this combination at too low a level; for their unity dwells in a place above the skies, outside this world.

Two things in Marx are solid, indestructible. One is the method which makes society an object of scientific study by seeking to define therein relationships of force; the other is the analysis of capitalist society as it existed in the nineteenth century. The rest not only is not true, but is even too inconsistent, too empty, to be called erroneous.

In omitting spiritual factors, Marx ran no risk of being greatly mistaken in his analysis of a society which, all in all, allotted them no place. At bottom, Marx's materialism only expressed the influence of this society upon him; his weakness lay in becoming himself the best instance of his own thesis concerning the subordination of thought to economic circumstances. But in his best moments he rose above this weakness. At such times materialism horrified him, and he would stigmatize it in the society of his time. He discovered a formula impossible to surpass when he said that the essence of capitalism lies in the subordination of subject to object, of man to thing. The analysis which he made of it from this point of view is of an incomparable vigour and depth; today still, today especially, it is an infinitely valuable theme for meditation.

But the general method is of still greater value. The idea of working out a mechanics of social relationships had been adumbrated by many lucid minds. It was doubtless this that inspired Machiavelli. As in ordinary mechanics, the fundamental notion would be that of force. The great difficulty is to grasp this notion.

Such an idea contains nothing incompatible with the purest spirituality; it is complementary to it. Plato compared society to a huge beast which men are forced to serve and which they are weak enough to worship. Christianity, so close to Plato on many points, contains not only the same thought, but the same image; the beast in the Apocalypse is sister to the great beast in Plato. Working out a social mechanics means, instead of worshipping the beast, to study its anatomy, physiology, reflexes, and, above all, to try to understand the mechanism of its conditioned reflexes, that is to say find a method for training it.

The essential idea in Plato—which is also that of Christianity, but has been very much neglected—is that man cannot escape being wholly enslaved to the beast, even down to the innermost recesses of his soul, except in so far as he is freed by the supernatural operation of grace. Spiritual servitude consists in confusing the necessary with the good; for "we do not know what a distance separates the essence of the necessary from that of the good".

The beast has one doctrine—that of force. Certain Athenians, whom Thucydides quotes, expressed it crudely, with a marvellous precision, when they said to some wretches imploring their mercy: "We believe as concerning the gods according to tradition, and we know as concerning men from unquestionable evidence, that each one always, through a necessity of nature, commands wherever he has the power to do so." It is clear that these Athenians were but recent converts to the cult of the beast, the descendants of men who had been strangers to it; the true worshippers of this cult do not reveal its doctrine, otherwise than by action. To justify such action they invent idolatries.

The reverse of this doctrine, with respect to the divinity, is the dogma of the Incarnation. "Who, being in the form of God, thought it not robbery to be equal with God: but made himself of no reputation, and took upon him the form of a servant . . . and became obedient unto death . . ."[1]

The beast is supreme on earth. The devil said to Christ: "All this power will I give thee, and the glory of them: for that is delivered unto me . . ."[2] The description of human societies purely in terms of relationships of force accounts for almost everything. The only thing it leaves out is the supernatural.

The share of the supernatural here below is secret, silent, almost invisible, infinitely small. But it is decisive. Proserpina did not think she was changing her destiny by eating just one pomegranate seed; yet from that moment, for ever after, the other world has been her home and her kingdom.

This decisive operation of the infinitely small is a paradox which the human intelligence finds it difficult to acknowledge. Through this paradox is accomplished the wise persuasion that Plato speaks of, that

[1] Philippians ii, 6–8.
[2] Luke iv, 6.

persuasion by means of which divine Providence induces necessity to direct most things towards the good.

Nature, which is a mirror of the divine truths, offers us everywhere an image of this paradox. Catalysts, bacteria are examples of it. Compared with a solid body, a point is something infinitely small. Yet, in each body, there is one point which predominates over the entire mass, for if the point is supported the body does not fall; that point is the centre of gravity.

But a point thus supported only prevents a mass from falling if the mass is disposed symmetrically around it, or if the asymmetry in it has certain proportions. Yeast only makes the dough rise if it is mixed with it. The catalyst only acts when in contact with the reactive elements. In the same way there exist certain material conditions for the supernatural operation of the divine that is present on earth in the form of something infinitely small.

The wretchedness of our condition subjects human nature to a moral form of gravity that is constantly pulling it downwards, towards evil, towards a total submission to force. "And God saw . . . that every imagination of the thoughts of his [man's] heart was only evil continually."[1] It is this gravity which forces man, on the one hand, to lose half his soul, according to an ancient proverb, the day he becomes a slave, and, on the other hand, to command always, according to the words quoted by Thucydides, wherever he has the power to do so. In the same way as ordinary gravity, it has its laws. When studying them, one cannot be too cold-blooded, lucid, cynical. In this sense, to this extent, one must be a materialist.

However, an architect not only studies falling bodies, but also the conditions for equilibrium. The true knowledge of social mechanics implies that of the conditions under which the supernatural operation of an infinitely small quantity of pure good, placed at the right point, can neutralize gravity.

Those who deny the reality of the supernatural truly resemble blind men. Light, too, exerts no pressure, has no weight; but by its means the plants and trees reach towards the sky in spite of gravity. We do not eat it; but the seeds and fruits that we eat would not ripen without it.

[1] Genesis vi, 5.

Similarly, the purely human virtues would not spring up out of man's animal nature without the supernatural light of grace. When man turns away from this light, a slow, progressive, but relentless decomposition finally subjects him altogether, right in the very depths of his soul, to the sway of force. As far as it is possible for a thinking creature, he becomes matter. In the same way a plant deprived of light is gradually changed into something inert.

Those who think that the supernatural, by definition, operates in an arbitrary fashion, incapable of being studied, are as wrong about it as are those who deny its reality. The true mystics, like St John of the Cross, describe the operation of grace on the soul with the precision of a chemist or a geologist. The influence of the supernatural on human societies, although perhaps still more mysterious, can no doubt also be studied.

If we examine closely not only the Middle Ages of Christendom, but all the really creative civilizations, we notice how each one, at any rate for a time, had at its very centre an empty space reserved for the purely supernatural, the reality that lies outside this world. Everything else was oriented towards this empty space.

There are not two methods of social architecture. There has never been more than one. It is eternal. But it is always the eternal which calls for a truly inventive effort on the part of the human spirit. This consists of disposing the blind forces of social mechanics around the point that also serves as centre for the blind forces of celestial mechanics, that is to say the "Love which moveth the sun and the other stars".

It is certainly no easy thing, either to conceive in a more precise manner or to accomplish. But at any rate the first condition for moving in this direction is to let one's thoughts dwell on it. It is not one of those things that can be obtained by accident. Maybe one can receive it after desiring it long and persistently.

The imitation of the order of the world was the great conception of pre-Roman antiquity. It should also have been the great conception behind Christianity, since the perfect model proposed for each man's imitation was the same being as the Wisdom ordering the universe. And in fact this conception did stir subterraneously the whole of the Middle Ages.

Today, after being bemused for several centuries with pride in technical achievement, we have forgotten the existence of a divine order of the universe. We do not realize that labour, art and science are only different ways of entering into contact with it.

If the humiliation produced by unhappiness were to rouse us, if we were to re-discover this great truth, we should be able to put an end to what constitutes the scandal of modern thought, the hostility between religion and science.

IS THERE A MARXIST DOCTRINE?

Many people declare themselves to be either opponents, or adherents, or qualified adherents of the Marxist doctrine. No one thinks of asking himself: Had Marx, in fact, a doctrine? One cannot imagine that something which has excited so much controversy might not exist. Yet such is frequently the case. The question is worth raising and examining. Perhaps, after an attentive examination, we shall find that a negative answer is called for.

It is generally agreed that Marx was a materialist. He was not always so at all stages of his career. As a young man, he had set out to work out a philosophy of labour in a spirit very closely akin, at bottom, to that of Proudhon. A philosophy of labour is not materialist. It arranges all the problems connected with man around an act which, constituting a direct and genuine grip on matter, contains man's relation to the opposing term. The opposing term is matter. Man is not reduced to it; he is placed in opposition to it.

Along this road, the youthful Marx did not even begin the sketch of a sketch. All he supplied were a few indications. Proudhon, for his part, only shed thereon a few flashes amid much smoke. Such a philosophy remains to be worked out. It is perhaps indispensable. It is perhaps more particularly a need of our time. There are a number of signs indicating that in the last century the germ of it was in process of formation. But nothing came of this. Possibly it is something that is reserved for our century to accomplish.

Marx was checked when still a young man by an accident very common in the nineteenth century; he began to take himself seriously. He was seized with a sort of messianic illusion which made him believe that he had been chosen to play a decisive role for the salvation of mankind. Thenceforward it was impossible for him to preserve the ability to think in the full sense of the word. He abandoned the philosophy of labour that was germinating in his mind, although he continued, less and less often as time went on, to include here and there in his writings formulas inspired by it. Being unable to work out a doctrine, he seized upon the two beliefs most current in his time, both of them meagre, superficial, mediocre and furthermore impossible to conceive in conjunction: the cult of science and utopian socialism.

In order to adopt them together, he gave them a fictitious unity by means of formulas which, if one enquires into their meaning, eventually fail to reveal any, except a sentimental state of mind. But when an author chooses his words with skill, the reader is rarely ungracious enough to raise such a question. The less meaning a formula possesses, the thicker is the veil drawn over the illegitimate contradictions of a line of thought.

This does not mean, of course, that Marx ever set out intentionally to deceive the public. The public he had to deceive in order to be able to live was himself. That is why he surrounded the basis of his conception with metaphysical clouds which, after one has looked at them fixedly for a certain length of time, become transparent, but reveal themselves to be empty.

However, he did not merely give a fictitious connection to the two systems that he had taken over ready-made, he also thought them out afresh. His mind, though of insufficient range to meet the requirements for creating a doctrine, was capable of ideas of genius. In his works there are compact fragments whose truth is unchanging, and which naturally have their place in any true doctrine. Thus it is that they are not only compatible with Christianity, but of infinite value to it. They must be taken back from Marx. This is all the easier in that what nowadays goes by the name of Marxism, that is to say the current of thought which claims to stem from Marx, makes no use of them at all. Truth is too dangerous to touch. It is an explosive.

The nineteenth-century cult of science consisted in the belief that the science of the period, by means of a simple development in certain directions already defined by the results achieved, would provide a definite answer to all the problems that could present themselves to man, without exception. What has, in fact, happened is that science, after expanding a little, has itself "cracked up". The science in favour today, although derived from the former, is a different science. Nineteenth-century science has been reverently deposited in the museum under the label "classical science".

It was well constructed, simple and homogeneous. Mechanics was its queen. Physics was its core. As this last was the branch in which by far the most brilliant results had been achieved, it naturally exercised considerable influence over all other studies. The idea of studying mankind in the same way as the physicist studies lifeless matter was bound thenceforth to impose itself, and was in fact extremely wide-spread. But man was hardly thought of except as an individual. Matter was now the flesh; or else there was an attempt to define a psycho-logical equivalent of the atom. Those who reacted against this obses-sion with the individual were also in reaction against the cult of science.

Marx was the first and, unless I am mistaken, the only one—for his researches were not followed up—to have the twin idea of taking society as the fundamental human fact and of studying therein, as the physicist does in matter, the relationships of force.

Here we have an idea of genius, in the full sense of the word. It is not a doctrine; it is an instrument of study, research, exploration and pos-sibly construction for every doctrine that is not to risk crumbling to dust on contact with a truth.

Having had this idea, Marx hastened to render it barren, as far as lay with him, by plastering over it the wretched cult of science of his time. Or rather, Engels, who was far inferior to him and knew it, performed this operation for him; but Marx covered it with his authority. The result was a system according to which the relationships of force that define the social structure entirely determine both man's destiny and his thoughts. Such a system is ruthless. Force counts for everything there; it leaves no hope for justice. It does not even leave the hope of conceiving justice in its truth, since all that thoughts do is to reflect the relationships of force.

But Marx was a generous soul. The sight of injustice made him suffer really, one might say in his flesh. This suffering was intense enough to have made it impossible for him to live had he not harboured the hope of an imminent and earthly reign of complete justice. For him, as for many, need was the best of proofs.

The majority of human beings do not question the truth of an idea without which they would literally be unable to live. Arnolphe did not question the faithfulness of Agnès. The supreme test for every soul is perhaps this choice between truth and life. Whosoever will save his life shall lose it. This sentence would be frivolous if it affected only those who under no circumstances are prepared to die. They are, in fact, quite rare. It becomes terrible when applied to those who refuse to part with the ideas—even should they be false—without which they feel themselves incapable of living.

The current conception of justice in Marx's day was that of the socialism which he himself named utopian. It was very poor in intellectual effort, but as a sentiment it was noble and humane, desiring liberty, dignity, well-being, happiness and every possible good for all. Marx adopted it. He attempted merely to give it greater precision, and so tacked some interesting ideas on to it, but nothing really of the first order.

What he did change was the character of hope. A probability based on human progress could not suffice him. To assuage his anguish, a certitude was necessary. You cannot base a certitude upon man. If the eighteenth century harboured this illusion at times—and it did so only at times—the upheavals caused by the French Revolution and war had been sufficiently appalling to cure men of it.

In previous centuries, those who required a certitude rested it on God. Eighteenth-century philosophy and the wonders of technical science seemed to have carried man to such heights that the habit of doing so had been lost. But later on, when the radical inadequacy of everything human began to be felt once more, it became necessary to seek for a support. God was out of fashion. So matter was taken. Man cannot bear for more than a moment to be alone in willing the good. He needs an all-powerful ally. If you do not believe in the remote, silent, secret omnipotence of a spirit, there remains only the manifest omnipotence of matter.

Herein lies the inevitable absurdity of all materialism. If the materialist could set aside all concern for the good, he would be perfectly consistent. But he cannot. The very being of man is nothing else but a perpetual straining after an unknown good. And the materialist is a man. That is why he cannot prevent himself from ultimately regarding matter as a machine for manufacturing the good.

The essential contradiction in human life is that man, with a straining after the good constituting his very being, is at the same time subject in his entire being, both in mind and in flesh, to a blind force, to a necessity completely indifferent to the good. So it is; and that is why no human thinking can escape from contradiction. Contradiction itself, far from always being a criterion of error, is sometimes a sign of truth. Plato knew this. But the cases can be distinguished. There is a legitimate and an illegitimate use of contradiction.

The illegitimate use lies in coupling together incompatible thoughts as if they were compatible. The legitimate use lies, first of all, when two incompatible thoughts present themselves to the mind, in exhausting all the powers of the intellect in an attempt to eliminate at least one of them. If this is impossible, if both must be accepted, the contradiction must then be recognized as a fact. It must then be used as a two-limbed tool, like a pair of pincers, so that through it direct contact may be made with the transcendental sphere of truth beyond the range of the human faculties. The contact is direct, though made through an intermediary, in the same way as the sense of touch is directly affected by the uneven surface of a table over which you pass, not your hand, but your pencil. The contact is real, though belonging to the number of things that by nature are impossible, for it is a case of a contact between the mind and that which is not thinkable. It is supernatural, but real.

There is an equivalent, an image as it were, very frequent in mathematics, of this legitimate use of contradiction as a means of reaching the transcendental. It plays an essential role in Christian dogma, as one can perceive with reference to the Trinity, the Incarnation, or any other example. The same applies to other traditions. It provides, perhaps, a criterion for discerning which religious and philosophical traditions are authentic.

It is, above all, the fundamental contradiction, that between the good and necessity, or its equivalent, that between justice and force, whose use constitutes a criterion. As Plato said, an infinite distance separates the good from necessity. They have nothing in common. They are totally other. Although we are forced to assign them a unity, this unity is a mystery; it remains for us a secret. The genuine religious life is the contemplation of this unknown unity.

The manufacture of a fictitious, mistaken equivalent of this unity, brought within the grasp of the human faculties, is at the bottom of the inferior forms of the religious life. To every genuine form of the religious life there corresponds an inferior form, which is based to all appearances on the same doctrine, but has no understanding of it. But the converse is not true. There are ways of thinking that are compatible only with a religious life of inferior quality.

In this respect the whole of materialism, in so far as it attributes to matter the automatic manufacture of the good, is to be classed among the inferior forms of the religious life. This is demonstrated even in the case of the bourgeois economists of the nineteenth century, the apostles of liberalism, who adopt a truly religious accent when they talk about production. It is demonstrated to a far greater degree still in the case of Marxism. Marxism is a fully-fledged religion, in the impurest sense of the word. In particular it shares in common with all inferior forms of the religious life the fact of having been continually used, according to Marx's perfectly accurate expression, as an opium of the people.

For that matter, only a shade of difference, something infinitely small, separates a spirituality like Plato's from materialism. He does not say that the good is an automatic product of necessity, but that the Spirit has domination over necessity through persuasion; it persuades necessity to cause most of the things that take place to turn towards the good, and necessity is overcome by means of this wise persuasion. Similarly, in the words of Aeschylus: "God does not arm himself with any violence. Everything that is divine is effortless. Dwelling on high, his wisdom yet succeeds in operating from thence, from his pure throne." We find the same conception in China, in India, in Christianity. It is expressed in the first line of the Lord's Prayer, which it would be better to translate: "Our Father, the one in heaven"; and even better by the wonderful words: "Your Father which is in secret."

The share of the supernatural here on earth is that of secrecy, silence, the infinitely small. But the operation of that something infinitely small is decisive. Proserpina did not think she was committing herself to anything when, yielding partly to constraint, partly to enticement, she consented to eat just one pomegranate seed; but from that moment, for ever after, the other world was her kingdom and her motherland. A pearl in a field can scarcely be seen. The grain of mustard seed is the smallest of all the seeds.

The decisive operation of the infinitely small is a paradox; the human intelligence has difficulty in acknowledging it; but nature, which is a mirror of the divine truths, everywhere presents us with images of it. Catalysts, bacteria, fermenting agents are examples. Compared with a solid body, a point is something infinitely small. Yet, in each body, there is one point which predominates over the entire mass, so that if that point receives support, the body does not fall. The keystone supports a whole building from above. Archimedes said: "Give me a point of leverage and I will lift the world." The silent presence of the supernatural here below is that point of leverage. That is why, in the early centuries of Christianity, the Cross was compared to a balance.

If an island completely cut off had never had any other than blind inhabitants, light would be for them what the supernatural is for us. One is tempted to think at first that for them it would be nothing, that by creating for their use a system of physics with all theory of light left out, one would be giving them a complete explanation of their world. For light offers no obstacle, exerts no pressure, is weightless, cannot be eaten. For them, it is absent. But it cannot be left out of account. By it alone the trees and plants reach towards the sky in spite of gravity. By it alone seeds, fruits, all the things we eat, are ripened.

In assigning a transcendental unity to the good and to necessity, one gives an incomprehensible solution to the fundamental human problem, especially when one adds thereto—as is indispensable—the still more incomprehensible belief that something of this transcendental unity is communicated to those who, without understanding it, without being able to make any use either of their intelligence or of their will in regard to it, contemplate it with love and desire.

That which escapes the human faculties cannot, by definition, be either verified or refuted. But consequences follow from it which are situated at the lower level, in the sphere accessible to our faculties; these consequences can be submitted to a verification. In point of fact, this test is successful. A second indirect verification arises out of universal consent. On the surface, the extreme variety of religions and philosophies would seem to indicate that this test is non-existent; this consideration has even led many minds into scepticism. But a closer examination reveals that, except in countries that have subordinated their spiritual life to imperialism, a mystic doctrine lies at the secret core of every religion; and although the mystic doctrines differ from each other, they are not only similar but absolutely identical as regards a certain number of essential points. A third indirect verification is inward experience. It is an indirect test, even for those who make the experiment, in the sense that it is an experience which escapes their faculties; they grasp only the exterior aspect of it and know it. Nevertheless, they also know its significance. Throughout past centuries there has been a very small number of human beings, obviously incapable not only of lying but also of self-deception, whose testimony in this matter is decisive.

These three tests are perhaps the only possible ones; but they are sufficient. One can add to them the equivalent of a *reductio ad absurdum* by examining the other solutions, those which manufacture a fictitious unity for the good and for necessity at the level of the human faculties. They give rise to absurd consequences, whose absurdity can be verified both by reasoning and by experience.

Among all these inadequate solutions, far the best, the most useful, the only ones perhaps which contain some fragments of pure truth, are the materialist solutions. Materialism accounts for everything, with the exception of the supernatural. This is no small gap, for in the supernatural everything is contained and infinitely surpassed. But if one leaves the supernatural out of account, one is right to be a materialist. This universe, minus the supernatural, is only matter. In describing it solely as matter, one seizes upon a particle of truth. In describing it as a combination of matter and of specifically moral forces belonging to this world, that are on a level with nature, one falsifies everything. That is why, for a Christian, Marx's writings are of much greater value than those, for example, of Voltaire and the Encyclopedists, who found a way of being atheists without being materialists. They were atheists, not only in the sense that they more or less definitely excluded all notion of a personal God—which is also the case with certain Buddhist sects that in spite of this have raised themselves up to the mystical life—but in the sense that they excluded everything which is not of this world. They believed—these simpletons—that justice is of this world. This forms the extremely dangerous illusion contained in what are called the principles of 1789, non-religious faith and so on.

Among all the forms of materialism, the works of Marx contain one extremely valuable indication, although he himself made hardly any real use of it, and his followers even less, much less—the idea of non-physical matter. Marx, rightly regarding society as being the human fact of primary importance in this world, directed his attention only to social matter; but one may similarly consider, in the second place, psychological matter; several trends in modern psychology point in this direction, although, unless I am mistaken, the notion of it has not been formulated. A certain number of current prejudices prevent this from being done.

The idea is this; it is indispensable to any well-founded doctrine; it is central. Under all the phenomena of a moral order, whether collective or individual, there is something analogous to matter properly so called. Something analogous; not matter itself. That is why the systems which Marx classified under what he called mechanical materialism, with a touch of justifiable disdain—systems which set out to explain the whole of human thought on the basis of a physiological mechanism—are nothing but nonsense. Thoughts are subject to a mechanism which is proper to themselves; but it is a mechanism. When we think of matter, we think of a mechanical system of forces subject to a blind and rigorous necessity. The same applies to that non-tangible matter which is the substance of our thoughts. Only it is very difficult to grasp therein the notion of force and to conceive the laws of this necessity.

However, even before arriving at that stage, it is already extremely useful to know that this specific necessity exists. It enables us to avoid two mistakes into which we are continually falling, for as soon as we get away from the one we fall into the other. The first is the belief that moral phenomena are exact copies of material phenomena; for example, that moral well-being results automatically and exclusively from physical well-being. The other is the belief that moral phenomena are arbitrary and can be brought about by auto-suggestion or suggestion from without, or indeed by an act of will.

They are not subject to physical necessity, but they are subject to necessity. They are exposed to the repercussion of physical phenomena, but it is a specific repercussion, in conformity with the specific laws of that necessity to which they are subject. Everything that is real is subject to necessity. There is nothing more real than the imagination; what is imagined is not real, but the state of mind in which imagining occurs is a fact. Given a certain state of imagining, this state can only be modified if the causes capable of producing such an effect are brought into play. These causes have no direct connection with the things imagined; but, on the other hand, they are not just anything. The relation between cause and effect is as rigorously determined in this field as it is in that of gravity. Only it is harder to know.

The mistakes made on this point are countless and are the cause of countless sufferings in daily life. For example, if a child says he isn't feeling well, is kept away from school, and all of a sudden finds the strength to play with some little friends, his indignant family think he has been lying. They say to him: "Since you had the strength to play, you had the strength to work". But the child may very well have been sincere. He was held back by a genuine feeling of exhaustion which the sight of his little friends and the attraction of playing with them have truly dissipated, whereas school lessons did not contain a sufficient stimulus to produce this effect. Similarly, it is naïve of us to be astonished when we firmly make a resolution and do not stick to it. Something stimulated us to make the resolution, but that something was not powerful enough to bring us to the point of carrying it out; what is more, the very act of making a resolution may have exhausted the stimulus and thus prevented even a start being made in carrying it out. This is what often happens when extremely difficult actions have to be undertaken. The well-known case of St Peter is probably an example.

This type of ignorance is continually stepping in to vitiate the relations between governments and peoples, between the ruling classes and the masses. For example, industrialists can only think of two ways of rendering their workers happy: either by raising their wages, or else by telling them they are happy and sacking the wicked communists who assure them to the contrary. They are unable to understand that, on the one hand, a workman's happiness consists above all in a certain attitude of mind towards his work; and that, on the other hand, this attitude of mind can be brought about only if certain objective conditions—impossible to know without making a serious study of the subject—have been fulfilled. This twin truth, suitably transposed, is the key to all the practical problems of human existence.

In the operation of this necessity which governs men's thoughts and actions, the relations between society and the individual are very complex. But the primacy of the social is obvious. Marx was right to begin by positing the reality of a social matter, of a social necessity, of whose laws one must at any rate have caught a glimpse before venturing to reflect on the destinies of the human race.

This idea was original in relation to his time; but, absolutely speaking, it is not original. Indeed, it is probable that no truth is really original. The true intention of Machiavelli, a man of genius, was probably to work out a mechanics of social relations. But much farther back Plato had the reality of social necessity constantly present in his mind.

Plato felt above all very strongly that social matter is an infinitely greater obstacle to overcome between the soul and the good than the flesh properly so called. That is also the Christian conception. St Paul says that we have to war not against the flesh, but against the devil; and the devil is on his own ground in social matter, since he was able to say to Christ, as he showed him the kingdoms of this world: "All this power will I give thee, and the glory of them: for that is delivered unto me . . ." That is why he is called the Prince of this world. Since he is the father of lies, this means, then, that social matter is the cultural and proliferating medium *par excellence* for lies and false beliefs. Such is certainly Plato's conception. He compared society to a huge beast which men are forced to serve and whose reflexes they study in order to derive therefrom their beliefs concerning good and evil. Christianity retained this image. The beast in the Apocalypse is sister to the one in Plato.

The central, fundamental conception in Plato—which is also a Christian conception—is that all men are absolutely incapable of having on the subject of good and evil opinions other than those dictated by the reflexes of the beast, except for predestined souls whom a supernatural grace draws towards God.

He did not develop this conception to any extent, although it is present behind all his writings, no doubt because he knew that the beast is wicked and revengeful. It provides a subject for reflection that is almost unexplored. Not that we have here a truth which is self-evident, far from it; it is very deeply hidden. It is hidden especially by conflicts of opinion. If two men are in violent disagreement about good and evil, it is hard to believe that both of them are blindly subject to the opinion of the society around them. In particular, he who ponders those few lines of Plato is very strongly tempted to attribute to the influence of the beast the opinions of those against whom he argues, while attributing his own to a correct view of justice and the good. But one has only understood the truth formulated by Plato when one has recognized it as true for oneself.

Actually at a given period, in a given social body, the differences of opinion are far fewer than it appears. There are far more conflicts than there are differences. The most violent struggles often divide people who think exactly, or almost exactly, the same thing. Our age is very fertile in paradoxes of this kind. The common fund whence spring the various trends of opinion at any given period is the opinion of the great beast at that period. For example, during the past ten years, every political tendency, including the very tiniest little groups, was accusing all the rest, without exception, of fascism, and having the same accusation levelled at it in return; except, of course, for those who regarded this epithet as a form of praise. Probably the epithet was always partially justified. The European great beast of the twentieth century has a pronounced taste for fascism. Another amusing example is the problem of coloured peoples. Each country waxes very sentimental over the wretched fate of those under the rule of other countries, but becomes highly indignant if any doubts are cast on the perfect happiness enjoyed by those under its own rule. There are many similar cases, in which the apparent difference between attitudes actually constitutes a sameness.

Furthermore, since the beast is huge and men are tiny, each one is differently placed in relation to it. Following up Plato's image, we may imagine that among those with the task of grooming it, one takes charge of a knee, another of a claw, another of the neck, another of the back. Perhaps it likes being tickled under the jaw and patted on the back. One of its attendants will consequently maintain that it is tickling which constitutes the supreme good; another that it is patting. In other words, society is composed of groups which interlock in all sorts of ways, and social morality varies from group to group. It would be impossible to find two individuals whose social backgrounds were truly identical; each man's background is composed of a network of groups which is nowhere else repeated in exactly the same way. Thus the apparent originality of individuals does not contradict the proposition that thought is completely subordinated to social opinion.

This proposition is the very one advanced by Marx. The only difference between him and Plato on this point is that he (Marx) is unaware of the possibility of exceptions brought about through the supernatural intervention of grace. This gap leaves the truth of a part of his researches quite intact, but is the reason why the rest is simply verbiage.

Marx sought to apprehend the mechanism of social opinion. The phenomenon of professional morality supplied him with the key to it. Every professional group manufactures a morality for itself in virtue of which the exercise of the profession, so long as it conforms to the rules, is quite outside the reach of evil. This is an almost vital need, for the stress of work, whatever it may be, is in itself so great that it would be unbearable if accompanied by anxious concern about good and evil. In order to protect oneself from this, armour is necessary. Professional morality fills this role.

For example, a doctor called upon to attend a man condemned to death will generally not ask himself the extremely agonizing question whether it is right to cure him. It is an accepted thing that doctors must try to cure their patients. Even for the slaves of Rome a particular morality was applicable, whereby a slave could do no wrong if acting in obedience to his master's orders or in his interests. Naturally, this morality was inculcated by the masters; but it was also largely adopted by the slaves, which is why the rebellions of slaves, considering their number and horrible misery, were rare. At the time when war was a profession, fighting men had a morality whereby any act of war, in accordance with the customs of war, and contributing to victory, was legitimate and right; including, for example, the violation of women or the killing of children when towns were sacked, for the licence given to the soldiers on these occasions was indispensable to maintain the morale of the army. Business has its own morality in which stealing is the blackest of crimes and any profitable exchange of an article for money legitimate and right. The characteristic common to all these moralities, and to every kinds of social morality, was formulated by Plato in definitive terms: "They call just and beautiful things that are necessary, for they do not know how great in reality is the distance which separates the essence of the necessary from that of the good."

Marx's conception is that the moral atmosphere of a given society—an atmosphere which permeates everywhere and combines with the morality peculiar to each social group—is itself composed of a mixture of group moralities whose dosage precisely reflects the amount of power exercised by each group. Thus, according as a society is ruled by great landed proprietors, or military men, or commercial men, or industrialists, or bankers, or bureaucrats, it will be wholly impregnated by the world conception bound up with the professional morality of such landed proprietors, military men, and so on. This world conception will everywhere find expression, in politics, in the laws, even in the abstract and apparently disinterested speculations of the intellectuals. Everyone will be governed by it, but no-one will be conscious of the fact, for each will think that it is a question, not of some particular conception, but of a way of thinking inherent in human nature.

All this is to a large extent true and easy to verify. To cite but one example, it is curious to note the importance attached to theft in the French penal code. When accompanied by certain aggravating circumstances, it is more severely punished than the rape of children. And yet the men who drew up this code not only had money, but also children whom no doubt they loved; if they had had to choose between losing a part of their wealth and having their children defiled, there is no reason to suppose that they would have preferred their money. But when drawing up the code they were, unbeknownst to themselves, simply the organs of social reflexes; and in a society based on commerce, theft is the prime anti-social act. Whereas the white slave traffic, for example, is a kind of commerce; that is why we have only with difficulty and half-heartedly brought ourselves to punish it.

So many facts, however, seem to contradict the theory that it would be refuted as soon as examined, were it not that it has to be qualified by the consideration of time. Man is a conservative creature, and there is a tendency for the past to subsist by its own weight. For instance, a considerable portion of the penal code dates from a time when commerce was much more important than it is today; thus, generally speaking, the moral atmosphere of a society contains elements originating among former ruling classes that have since disappeared or more or less fallen into decay. But the converse is true also. Just as a head of the opposition, destined to become one day prime minister, already has a following, so a more or less feeble class, but one destined soon to rule, already has around it an outline of the ideological trend that will dominate with and through it. It is in this way that Marx explained the socialism of his period, including the phenomenon Marx. He saw himself as the swallow which by its mere presence announces the near approach of spring, that is to say of the revolution. He was a portent for and of himself.

The second step in his explanatory attempt consisted of a search for the mechanism of social power. This part of his thought is extremely feeble. He thought he could affirm that the relationships of force in a given society, if traces of the past are excluded, depend entirely on the technical conditions of production. These conditions being given, a society has the structure which makes the maximum production possible. In trying continually to produce more and more, it improves the conditions of production. Thus these conditions change. A moment comes when a break in continuity takes place, as when water that is being gradually heated suddenly starts to boil. The new conditions make a new structure necessary. An effective change-over of power occurs, followed, after a certain interval marked by more or less violent manifestations, by the corresponding political, legal and ideological changes. When the manifestations are violent, this is called a revolution.

There is a right conception here, but, by a strange irony, it flatly contradicts Marx's own political standpoint: it is that a visible revolution never takes place except to sanction an invisible revolution already accomplished. When a social class noisily seizes power, it is because it already silently possessed that power, at any rate to a very large extent; otherwise it would not have the strength necessary to seize it. It is an obvious fact, from the moment one regards society as being governed by relationships of force. This is clearly evidenced by the French Revolution, which, as Marx himself showed, officially handed over to the bourgeoisie the power which it already possessed in fact, at any rate since the time of Louis XIV. It is further evidenced by recent revolutions which, in several countries, have placed the whole of national life under the power of the State. Before this, the State already played a vast role and was almost everything.

The plain consequence to be drawn, it seems, for a partisan of the workers' revolution is that, before launching the workers into the adventure of a political revolution, one must try to find out if methods exist likely to enable them to lay hold silently, gradually, almost invisibly, of a considerable part of real social power; and that one must either apply these methods if they exist, or give up the idea of a workers' revolution if they do not. But obvious as this consequence is, Marx did not perceive it, and that because he could not face it without losing what was for him his reason for living. For the same reason, his disciples, whether reformists or revolutionaries, were in no danger of seeing it. That is why it is possible to say, without fear of exaggeration, that as a theory of the workers' revolution Marxism is a nullity.

The rest of his theory of social transformations is based on a number of foolish misapprehensions. The first consists in adopting, in the case of human history, Lamarck's explanatory principle "the function creates the organ", the principle whereby the giraffe is supposed to have made such efforts to eat bananas that its neck has been lengthened. It is the type of explanation which, without containing so much as the beginning of an indication for the solution of a problem, gives the false impression that it has been solved, and thus prevents it from being posed. The problem is to discover how it is the organs of animals find themselves adapted to needs; by bringing forward as an answer the supposition of a tendency to adaptation inherent in animal life, you fall into the error ridiculed for all time by Molière in connection with the dormitive virtue of opium.

Darwin cleaned up the problem thanks to the simple and brilliant idea of conditions of existence. It is surprising that there should be animals on the earth. But once there are, it is not surprising that there should be a correspondence between their organs and their requirements for living, for otherwise they would not live. There is no chance whatever that anyone will ever discover in some remote corner of the world a species whose exclusive diet is bananas, but which is prevented by an unfortunate physical malformation from eating them.

Here is one of those all-too-obvious pieces of evidence which nobody sees until some inspired intuition makes them manifest. In actual fact, this one had been recognized by the Greeks, as is the case with almost all our ideas; but it had afterwards been forgotten. Darwin was a contemporary of Marx. But Marx, like all scientists, was very much behindhand in matters of science. He thought he was doing a scientist's work in purely and simply transferring Lamarck's naïve ideas to the social sphere.

He even introduced an additional arbitrary element by assuming that the function not only creates an organ capable of carrying it out, but further, roughly speaking and on the whole, the organ capable of doing so with the highest possible degree of efficiency. His sociology is based on postulates which, when submitted to the examination of reason, are found to be invalid, and which, when compared with the facts, are manifestly false.

He assumes in the first place that, given the technical conditions of production, society possesses the structure capable of using them to the maximum. Why? By virtue of what necessity should things take place in such a way that productive capacity is utilized to the maximum? In point of fact, no one has any idea of what that maximum may be. It is only clear that there has always been a good deal of waste in all societies. But this idea of Marx's is based on such vague notions that one cannot even show that it is false, for lack of the ability to grasp it.

Secondly, society is assumed to be continually endeavouring to improve production. This is the postulate of the liberal economists transferred from the individual to society as a whole. It can be accepted with reservations; but, in fact, there have been many societies in which for centuries people thought only of living as their forefathers had lived before them.

Thirdly, this effort is assumed to react on the actual conditions of production, and that always in such a way as to improve them. If one applies reasoning to this assertion, it is seen to be arbitrary; if one compares it with the facts, it is seen to be false. There is no reason at all why in trying to make the conditions of production furnish a greater yield they must always be developed. One can just as easily exhaust them. That very often takes place—in the case of a mine or a field, for example. The same phenomenon occurs, from time to time, on a grand scale, and provokes great crises. It is the story of the hen with the golden eggs. Aesop knew far more about that subject than Marx.

Fourthly, when this improvement has gone beyond a certain point, the social structure, which previously was the most efficient from the production point of view, is no longer so; and, according to Marx, this fact alone necessarily results in society abandoning that structure and adopting another as efficient as possible.

This is the height of arbitrary reasoning. It does not withstand a minute's close examination. Certainly, of all the men who have taken part in political, social or economic changes in past centuries, not one has ever said to himself: "I am going to bring about a change in the social structure in order that present productive capacity may be utilized to the maximum." Nor can one discern the least sign of any automatic mechanism which would result from the laws of social necessity and set going a transformation when productive capacity was not being fully utilized. Neither Marx nor the Marxists have ever furnished the slightest indication in this sense.

Must we therefore suppose that behind human history there is an all-powerful spirit, a wisdom that watches over the course of events and directs it? In that case Marx would seem to accept, without saying so, the truth recognized by Plato. There is no other way of accounting for his conception. But it remains bizarre all the same. Why should this hidden spirit watch over the interests of production? Spirit is what tends towards the good. Production is not the good. The nineteenth-century industrialists were alone in confusing the two. The hidden spirit which directs the destinies of the human race is, however, not that of a nineteenth-century industrialist.

The explanation is that the nineteenth century was obsessed by production, and especially the progress of production, and that Marx was slavishly subject to the influence of his age. This influence made him forget that production is not the good. He also forgot that it is not the only necessity, and this is the cause of a further foolishness—the belief that production is the sole factor in relationships of force. Marx purely and simply forgets war. The same thing happened to the majority of his contemporaries. The men of the nineteenth century, while gorging themselves on Béranger's songs and Epinal pictures in praise of Napoleon, had almost forgotten the existence of war. Marx once thought of briefly indicating that the methods of warfare depend on the conditions of production; but he did not perceive the converse relationship whereby the conditions of production are governed by the methods of warfare. Man can be threatened with death, either by nature or by his fellow man, and force, in the final analysis, comes down to the threat of death. When considering relationships of force, one must always think of force under its two-fold aspect of material need and of arms.

The result of this oversight on Marx's part has been a ridiculous confusion in Marxist circles, when confronted with war and the problems relating to war and peace. There is absolutely nothing in what is called Marxist doctrine to indicate the attitude a Marxist should adopt in regard to these problems. For a time like ours, it is a quite serious lacuna.

The only form of war Marx takes into consideration is social war—open or underground—under the name of the class struggle. He even makes of it the sole principle for explaining history. Since, on the other hand, the development of production is also the sole principle of historical development, it must be supposed that these two phenomena form but one. But Marx does not say how each can be reduced to the other. Certainly the oppressed who revolt or the inferiors who want to become superiors never entertain the thought of increasing society's productive capacity. The only connection one can imagine is that men's permanent protest against the social hierarchy maintains society in the requisite state of fluidity for productive forces to shape it at will.

In that case, the class struggle is not an active principle, but merely a negative condition. The active principle remains that mysterious spirit which watches over the maintenance of production at the maximum level, and which Marxists sometimes refer to, in the plural, as the productive forces. They take this mythology with the utmost seriousness. Trotsky wrote that the 1914–18 war was in reality a revolt of the productive forces against the limitations of the capitalist system. One may ponder for a long time over such a pronouncement, wondering what it means, until one is forced to admit that it has no meaning.

Yet Marx was right in regarding the love of liberty and the love of domination as the two motive-springs which keep social life in a permanent state of unrest. Only he forgot to prove that that is a materialist principle of explanation. It is not self-evident. The love of liberty and the love of domination are two human facts which can be interpreted in several different ways.

Furthermore, these two facts have a far wider bearing than the relation of oppressed to oppressor, which alone held Marx's attention. You cannot make use of the notion of oppression without having first made a serious effort to define it, for it is not clear. Marx did not take the trouble to do this. The selfsame men are oppressed in certain respects, oppressors in certain other respects; or again may desire to become so, and this desire can override the desire for liberty; and the oppressors, for their part, think far less often about keeping those under them obedient than of getting the better of their equals. Thus there is not the counterpart of a battle with two sides opposing each other, but rather an extraordinarily complicated tangle of guerilla forces. This tangle is nevertheless governed by laws. But they remain to be discovered.

Marx's only real contribution to social science lies in the submission that such a science is needed. That is already a good deal; it is in fact immense; but we are still where he left us. This science is still needed. Marx did not even get ready to begin to establish it. Much less his followers. In the term "scientific socialism", which is Marxism's own way of describing itself, the epithet "scientific" corresponds to nothing but a fiction. One would even be tempted to say more crudely a lie; only that Marx and the majority of his followers did not intend to lie. If these men had not been in the first place their own dupes, one would have to designate as a swindle the operation by which they have converted to their own exclusive benefit the respect felt for science by the men of today.

Marx was incapable of any real effort of scientific thought, because that did not interest him. All this materialist was interested in was justice. He was obsessed by it. His admirably clear view of social necessity was of a kind to plunge him into despair, since it is a necessity powerful enough to prevent men, not only from obtaining, but even from conceiving justice. He did not want anything to do with despair. He felt in himself, irresistibly, that man's desire for justice is too deeply implanted to admit of a refusal. He took refuge in a dream wherein social matter itself takes charge of the two functions that it denies man, namely, not only to accomplish justice, but to conceive it.

He labelled this dream "dialectical materialism". This was sufficient to shroud it in mystery. These two words are of an almost impenetrable emptiness. A very amusing game—though rather a cruel one—is to ask a Marxist what they mean.

All the same, by searching hard, one can discover a sort of meaning in them. Plato named dialectics that movement of the soul which, at each stage, in order to rise to the sphere above, leans for support on the irreducible contradictions of the sphere wherein it finds itself. At the end of this ascent, it is in contact with the absolute good.

Contradiction in matter is imaged by the clash of forces coming from different directions. Marx purely and simply attributed to social matter this movement towards the good through contradictions, which Plato described as being that of the thinking creature drawn upwards by the supernatural operation of grace.

It is easy to see how he was led to this. To begin with, he adopted unreservedly the two false beliefs to which the bourgeois of his time clung so hard: first, the confusion between production and the good, and consequently between the progress of production and progress towards the good; and secondly, the arbitrary generalization by which the progress of production—so strongly felt in the nineteenth century—is made the permanent law of human history.

Only, as opposed to the bourgeois, Marx was not happy. The thought of human misery distressed him terribly, as it does anyone who is not insensitive. He needed, by way of compensation, something catastrophic, a striking act of revenge, a punishment. He could not visualize progress as a continuous movement. He saw it as a series of violent, explosive shocks. It is certainly useless to ask oneself which was right, the bourgeoisie or he. This very notion of progress in favour during the nineteenth century is devoid of meaning.

The Greeks used the word "dialectics" when thinking of the virtue of contradiction as support for the soul drawn upwards by grace. Since Marx, for his part, combined the material image of contradiction with the material image of the soul's salvation, namely, the clashes between forces and the progress of production, he was perhaps right to use this word "dialectics". But, on the other hand, this word, when coupled with the word "materialism", immediately shows up the absurdity of the idea. If Marx did not feel it, that was because he borrowed the word, not from the Greeks, but from Hegel, who was already using it without any precise meaning. As for the public, it was in no danger of being shocked; Greek thought is no longer a sufficiently living thing for that. On the contrary, the words were very suitably chosen so as to lead people to say to themselves: "That must mean something". When readers or listeners have been brought to that state, they are very open to suggestion.

Formerly, in adult education centres for the people, workers used sometimes to say, with a sort of timid eagerness, to intellectuals calling themselves Marxists: "We should very much like to know what dialectical materialism is". There is little likelihood that they were ever satisfied.

As for the mechanism of the automatic production of the absolute good through social conflicts, there is no difficulty in grasping what Marx's conception of it was; all that is very superficial.

Since the origin of social lies is to be found among the groups struggling for domination or emancipation, the disappearance of such groups would abolish lies, and man would live in justice and in truth. And what is the mechanism by which these groups can be made to disappear? It is very simple. Every time there is a social transformation, the dominant group falls and a relatively lower group takes its place. One has only to generalize; the whole of the science, and even the thought, of the nineteenth century, suffered from that vicious habit of uncontrolled extrapolation; except in the case of mathematics, the idea of limit was almost unknown. If each time a group lower in the scale attains to the dominant position, one day the lowest of all will do so; thenceforth there will be no more inferiors, no more oppression, no longer a social structure composed of hostile groups, no longer any lies. Men will possess justice, and because they possess it, they will know it as it is.

It is thus that we must understand the passages in which Marx seems completely to exclude the very notions of justice, truth or good. So long as justice is absent, man cannot conceive it, and *a fortiori* he cannot become possessed of it; it can only come to him from outside. Since society is vitiated, poisoned, and the social poison permeates all men's thoughts without exception, everything that men imagine under the name of justice is simply lies. Anyone who talks of justice, truth, or no matter what type of moral value, is a liar or allows himself to be hoodwinked by liars. How, then, is one to serve justice, if one does not know it? The only way to do so, according to Marx, is to hasten forward the operation of that mechanism, inherent in the very structure of social matter, which will automatically bring men justice.

It is difficult really to be sure whether Marx thought that the role of the proletariat in this mechanism, by putting it closer to the future society, communicated to it and to the writers or militants who ranged themselves on its side an initial glimpse, as it were, of the truth, or whether he regarded the proletariat simply as a blind instrument of that entity which he named "history". It is probable that his thoughts fluctuated on this point. But it is certain that he regarded the proletariat, together with its allies and leaders brought in from outside, above all as an instrument.

He regarded as just and good, not that which appears to be so to minds warped by the social lie, but solely that which could hasten the appearance of a society without lies; on the other hand, in this field, everything which is effective, without exception, is perfectly just and good, not in itself, but relatively to the final goal.

Thus in the end Marx fell back into that group morality which revolted him to the point of making him hate society. Like the feudal magnates of old, like the business men of his own day, he had built for himself a morality which placed above good and evil the activity of the social group to which he belonged, that of professional revolutionaries.

This is what always happens. The type of moral failing that we most fear and hate, that fills us with the greatest horror, is invariably the one into which we fall, when we do not seek the source of the good in the place where it dwells. It is the snare perpetually laid for each man, and against which there is but one protection.

This mechanism for producing paradise imagined by Marx is something obviously puerile. Force is a relationship; the strong are so in relation to those weaker than themselves. It is impossible for the weak to take possession of social power; those who take possession of social power by force always form—even before this operation—a group to which human masses are subjected. Marx's revolutionary materialism consists in positing, on the one hand that everything is exclusively regulated by force, and on the other that a day will suddenly come when force will be on the side of the weak. Not that certain ones who were weak will become strong—a change that has always taken place; but that the entire mass of the weak, while continuing to be such, will have force on its side.

If the absurdity of this does not immediately strike us, it is because we think that number is a force. But number is a force in the hands of him who disposes of it, not in the hands of those who go to make it up. Just as the energy contained in coal is a force only after having passed through a steam engine, so the energy contained in a human mass is a force only for a group outside the mass, much smaller than the mass, and having established with it relations which, as a result of very close study, could perhaps be defined. It follows from this that the force of the mass is used on behalf of interests which are exterior to it, exactly as the force of an ox is used in the interests of the ploughman, or that of a horse in the interests of the rider. Someone may knock the rider off and jump into the saddle in his place, then get knocked off in his turn; this may be repeated a hundred or a thousand times; the horse will still have to keep on running under the prick of the spur. And if the horse unseats the rider, another will quickly take his place.

Marx was perfectly well aware of all this; he set it forth brilliantly in connection with the bourgeois State; but he wanted to forget it when it came to the revolution. He knew that the mass is weak and only constitutes a force in the limits of others; for, were it otherwise, there would never have been oppression. He let himself be persuaded solely by generalization, by applying the limiting process to that perpetual change which periodically sets those who were weaker in the place of those who were stronger. The limiting process, when applied to a relation one of whose terms it eliminates, is altogether too absurd. But this wretched form of reasoning sufficed for Marx, because anything suffices to persuade the man who feels that, if he were not persuaded, he could not live.

The idea that weakness as such, while remaining weak, can constitute a force, is not a new one. It is the Christian idea itself, and the Cross is the illustration of it. But it has to do with a force of quite a different kind from that wielded by the strong; it is a force that is not of this world, that is supernatural. It operates after the manner of the supernatural, decisively, but secretly, silently under the aspect of the infinitely small; and if it penetrates the masses by radiation, it does not dwell in them, but in certain souls. Marx accepted this contradiction of strength in weakness, without accepting the supernatural which alone renders the contradiction valid.

Similarly, Marx sensed a truth, an essential truth, when he realized that man can conceive justice only if he has . . .

(*Here the manuscript, written in London in 1943, breaks off.*)

Routledge Classics
Get inside a great mind

The Need for Roots
Simone Weil

'This is one of those books which ought to be studied by the young before their leisure has been lost and their capacity for thought destroyed; books the effect of which, we can only hope, will become apparent in the attitude of mind of another generation.'
T. S. Eliot

Written in the last year of her life, Simone Weil's *The Need for Roots* is a powerful denunciation of the false values of contemporary civilization, setting out a radical vision for spiritual and political renewal to combat a dehumanizing cult of materialism. The book has become an enduring spiritual testament for our age and is the extraordinary final work of one of the most original thinkers of the twentieth century, who possessed, as T. S. Eliot commented, a 'genius akin to saints'.

Hb: 0–415–27101–0   Pb: 0–415–27102–9

Modern Man in Search of a Soul
Carl Gustav Jung

'He was more than a psychological or scientific phenomenon; he was to my mind one of the greatest religious phenomena the world has ever experienced.'
Laurens van der Post

Modern Man in Search of a Soul is the perfect introduction to the theories and concepts of one of the most original and influential religious thinkers of the twentieth century. Lively and insightful, it covers all his most significant themes, including man's need for a God and the mechanics of dream analysis. One of his most famous books, it perfectly captures the feelings of confusion that many sense today.

Hb: 0–415–25544–9   Pb: 0–415–25390–X

For these and other classic titles from Routledge, visit
www.routledgeclassics.com

Some titles not available in North America

Routledge Classics
Get inside a great mind

The Fear of Freedom
Erich Fromm

'Erich Fromm speaks with wisdom, compassion, learning and insight into the problems of individuals trapped in a social world that is needlessly cruel and hostile.'
Noam Chomsky

Erich Fromm sees right to the heart of our contradictory needs for community and for freedom like no other writer before or since. In *The Fear of Freedom*, Fromm warns that the price of community is indeed high, and it is the individual who pays. He leaves a valuable and original legacy to his readers – a vastly increased understanding of the human character in relation to society.

Hb: 0–415–25542–2   Pb: 0–415–25388–8

The Gift
with a foreword by Mary Douglas
Marcel Mauss

'The teaching of Marcel Mauss was one to which few can be compared. No acknowledgement of him can be proportionate to our debt.'
Claude Lévi-Strauss

In this seminal work, Michael Mauss utterly revolutionized our understanding of the process of exchange thereby calling into question the rationale behind society's most cherished assumptions. In a world increasingly obsessed by runaway consumption *The Gift* has never been of greater relevance and, as Lévi-Strauss remarked, few can read this book without feeling that they are somehow 'present at a decisive event in the evolution of science.'

Hb: 0–415–26748–X   Pb: 0–415–26749–8

For these and other classic titles from Routledge, visit
www.routledgeclassics.com